# Backward Glances

# Backward Glances

## Exploring Italy,
## Reinterpreting America (1831–1866)

## Leonardo Buonomo

**Madison • Teaneck**
**Fairleigh Dickinson University Press**
**London: Associated University Presses**

© 1996 by Associated University Presses, Inc.

All rights reserved. Authorization to photocopy items for internal or personal use, or the internal or personal use of specific clients, is granted by the copyright owner, provided that a base fee of $10.00, plus eight cents per page, per copy is paid directly to the Copyright Clearance Center, 222 Rosewood Drive, Danvers, Massachusetts 01923. [0-8386-3649-7/96 $10.00 + 8¢ pp, pc.]

Associated University Presses
440 Forsgate Drive
Cranbury, NJ 08512

Associated University Presses
25 Sicilian Avenue
London WC1A 2QH, England

Associated University Presses
P.O. Box 338, Port Credit
Mississauga, Ontario
Canada L5G 4L8

The paper used in this publication meets the requirements
of the American National Standard for Permanence of Paper
for Printed Library Materials Z39.48–1984.

**Library of Congress Cataloging-in-Publication Data**

Buonomo, Leonardo
    Backward glances : exploring Italy, reinterpreting America : 1831–1866 /
Leonardo Buonomo.
        p.  cm.
    Includes bibliographical references and index.
    ISBN 0-8386-3649-7 (alk. paper)
    1. American literature--Italian influences. 2. American literature--19th century--
History and criticism. 3. Travelers' writings, American--History and criticism. 4.
Americans Travel--Italy History--19th century. 5. Italy--In literature. I. Title.
PS159.I8B86    1996
810.9'3245--dc20                                                95-10317
                                                                    CIP

PRINTED IN THE UNITED STATES OF AMERICA

*For my parents
in love and gratitude*

# Contents

7

# Acknowledgments

I wish to express my deepest appreciation to Roy Harvey Pearce and Andrew Wright for their encouragement, advice, and criticism. I am also particularly grateful to William Boelhower for his support, guidance, and friendship. My thanks for help in particular ways go also to Gabrielle Barfoot, H. Stuart Hughes, Stephanie H. Jed, Simonetta Pelusi, Don E. Wayne, and Rosella Mamoli Zorzi.

Portions of chapters 1 and 4 appeared in somewhat different form in the academic publication of the University of Venice *Annali di Ca' Foscari*.

# Introduction

Throughout the nineteenth century, a great number of American artists — mostly painters, sculptors, and writers — abandoned their cities and the familiarity of their social sphere to embark on a long and often perilous journey to Europe. Their sojourn in the Old World almost always lasted several months, sometimes a number of years, and in some cases the continent was even elected as a place of residence for the remainder of one's lifetime. The favorite destinations in Europe were England and Italy. The two countries represented equally powerful, but quite different, sources of attraction for American travelers. England offered them the pleasure of a familiar past, of a renewed contact with their cultural heritage. Italy, in addition to its widely recognized reputation as homeland of the arts, possessed to their eyes the irresistible charm of the exotic. Not at all awed, but rather stimulated by the alien quality of Italy's traditions and customs, many visitors from the United States gave themselves the task of writing down that foreign reality for their countrymen.

It is with some of the results of their creative efforts that this study is mainly concerned. It undertakes to explore the ways in which Italy was portrayed in a number of nineteenth-century works by both major and minor American writers. It intends to show, moreover, how these authors, while writing about Italy, were also writing about the United States; while striving to define the new scene in front of them, they were also, more or less consciously, defining what they had left behind.

I have chosen to concentrate on works written before Italy's achievement of independence and political unity (1870), as the difficulties confronting American writers residing there before that event were very different from, and greater than, those encountered by later visitors. Before 1870, any description or narrative use of Italy was in fact an attempt to come to terms with what was contemptuously referred to as a mere geographical denomination.[1] The spectacle of a country ruled in part by foreign forces and aspiring to self-determination was potentially rich in emotional associations for American observers. They found themselves confronted, in fact, with a sort of reenactment of the making of America's own nationhood. Yet not all the Americans who wrote about Italy in these years recognized this link, and some of those who did recognize it chose not to deal with it in their writings. Their different attitudes need to be considered carefully; they may tell us a good deal about the sojourners' sentiments toward both Italy and the United States. They may tell us, perhaps, that the travelers were satisfied with the state of things in their country of birth. Or, on the contrary, that they saw the current evolution of the United States as a moving away from the nation's democratic origins.

The seven texts examined in this study — James Fenimore Cooper's *The Bravo* (1831), Henry T. Tuckerman's *The Italian Sketchbook* (1835), Margaret Fuller's travel letters for *The New York Tribune* (1847–49), Julia Ward Howe's "Italian poems" in *Passion Flowers* (1854), Nathaniel Hawthorne's *The Marble Faun* (1860), Henry P. Leland's *Americans in Rome* (1863), and William Dean Howells's *Venetian Life* (1866) — were chosen because they document their authors' Italian experience. They are representative of a variety of literary forms: from journalism to prose fiction, from poetry to thinly disguised autobiography. Only some of these works — those of Fuller, Howells, and parts of Tuckerman's — correspond accurately enough to what is possibly the most familiar type of "récit de voyage": the realistic account of one's experience abroad. The others reinvent and interpret such an experience through characters and plot or lyrical expression. The term "travel literature," as used in this study, includes both these categories.

As the titles show, I deliberately selected only works that were intended for the public (hence the preference, for example, of Fuller's letters for the *Tribune* over her private correspondence), as I am particularly interested in the question of authorial responsibility that such destination inevitably comports. These writers were in fact certainly aware that a large part of their American audience would not have an opportunity to balance what they read about Italy with their own impressions. For the majority of readers, who only traveled vicariously through books and newspapers, the Italy described on the printed page was the only

Italy they were ever to know, the only real Italy. In relation to the above-mentioned works, this anonymous mass of readers functions very much like an invisible character whose presence can somehow be constantly sensed.

Several studies of nineteenth-century American writers' Italian experiences concentrate on the theme of art. They guide us through Italy's cities, churches, and ruins, or they make us pause in front of renowned pictures and statues, attempting to analyze the impact of such scenes on early visitors from the New World. If the emphasis is on the description of Italian life, however, historical reconstruction gives way to textual analysis. The critic's attention is likely to focus on private letters and journals — those texts, that is, which may best illuminate the biographical aspects of the author's Italian sojourn. And when a writer's correspondence, notes, or diaries are examined alongside his or her Italian novels or stories, the aim is usually to identify the motives behind particular stylistic or narrative choices.

What I propose for my diversified selection of works is a critical approach that combines textual comment with considerations of ethnographic character. I believe that texts as dissimilar as *The Bravo*, Fuller's dispatches, and Howe's poems served exactly the same "functions" for their American audience: they were all literary representations of nineteenth-century Italy and "official" descriptions of the local culture. For the common reader who had no access to "private writings," they were the only documentary evidence of the writers' observation of the Italian scene. They were the visible and tangible result of the exploration of a different world, of the study of different customs. To read them as such today gives us then the chance to find in their narration and description of Italy valuable insights into the mechanisms and strategies of cultural interpretation.

The number of American texts dealing in one way or another with Italy in the years I am examining is conspicuous. It includes writings by both "professional" men and women of letters (such as Washington Irving, Henry Wadsworth Longfellow, and Harriet Beecher Stowe) and artists whose chief mode of expression was painting or sculpture (as, for instance, Washington Allston, Horatio Greenough, and William Wetmore Story). These works form a corpus of ideas, impressions, and approaches from which it is possible to draw a series of broad considerations. What follows here is a purposely general panorama of American views of Italy.

It is a presentation of themes and questions that may help to set the works discussed in the following chapters in the appropriate context.

Whether they stated it openly or not, most Americans who wrote about Italy during the nineteenth century attempted to elaborate a definition of the local culture and character. Novelists, poets, and art critics turned into amateur ethnographers and set out to record their observations and analyses of foreign customs. They did it — in the majority of cases — in spite of a serious impediment to the effectiveness and accuracy of such research, namely: a scarce acquaintance with Italian language, traditions, history, and literature. They did it, what is more, in a country traditionally characterized by a multiplicity of customs and idioms. Italy's cultural fragmentation, however less conspicuous since the advent of the television era, has survived to this day (finding expression, for example, in the electoral success of the Northern League — a political party that advocates federalism — and in the title of a recent best-selling volume: Giorgio Bocca's *La dis-unità d'Italia* [The dis-unity of Italy], 1990). Nonetheless, the fact that these writers disregarded objective difficulties in their desire to portray a foreign reality should not be simply dismissed as evidence of presumption or superficiality. Notwithstanding their methodological weakness, such efforts to describe otherness seem to me of great interest as possible symptoms of the writers' insecurity about their own cultural identity.

In describing Italy and comparing it with their native country, most Americans emphasized differences rather than similarities. Differentiating themselves, they also defined — or redefined — themselves. As Francesco Remotti has observed, the classification of others signals the formative moment of any society (1990, 28), and Italy, for America, functioned as a perfect Other. Italy was the site of antiquity and Catholicism. It was, furthermore, divided into a number of small states whose governments seemed to be based on the antithesis of democracy. Finally, its life seemed to be characterized by a pervasive devotion to aestheticism.

The awareness of one's cultural distinctiveness that comes through "the experience of otherness" (to use Peter Kuon's expression [1987, 188]) was not the only advantage of a journey through Italy. Authors could also acquire a flattering view of their work as a mission, their pen assuming the mythical character of an instrument of preservation. In a good number of American books on Italy, one detects in fact a certain apprehensive concern for the survival of the country's "picturesque" quality. Aspects of Italian life perceived as quaint and old-fashioned, as remnants of distant epochs, might be saved for posterity by being crystallized in the text. Such a concept of writing may be associated, in my view, with what James Clifford has called "salvage, or redemptive, ethnography," or writing characterized by paternalistic undertones (the author assumes that the other society "'needs' to be represented by an outsider") (1986, 113).

Admittedly, the case to which Clifford refers specifically — that of an observer dealing with a culture that does not express itself through writing — seems at first hardly comparable to those examined in this study. Yet, in relation to those traits of Italian life seen by foreigners as curious or outlandish, the whole local population may be said to have been, in a sense, illiterate, i.e., unable to represent itself, for even the restricted, learned elite, which was sufficiently skilled to record in writing the country's reality, would invariably ignore the picturesque. They would fail to register it because to their eyes it was not a remarkable element of the scene.

"Redemptive ethnography," Clifford believes, presupposes that "what matters" in the other society's life "is its past, not present or future" (1986, 113). This emphasis on the past, this nostalgia (which sometimes is a sign of appreciation for the originality of a civilization), may betray a disturbing indifference toward the object of one's study. In the specific case of nineteenth-century Italy, the impression is, at times, that what is depicted by certain American writers is not a country inhabited by real people, with concrete — perhaps prosaic — problems and needs. It is rather a gigantic picture, or a stage where a performance is continually held for the sake of a foreign audience. In *Orientalism* (1991), Edward Said uses the image of the stage to describe the way both Europeans and Americans have traditionally viewed Eastern and Arab cultures. In applying it to nineteenth-century Italy, I wish to suggest that for many foreign visitors the country functioned as a relatively accessible and not too disquieting Orient. Describing what takes place on that stage, authors express their reaction to what they see, their appreciation or displeasure, and, more often than not, maintain a distance that is typical of the spectator. The sense of comfort, of reassurance that derives from such a distance, is what ultimately prevails over any other feeling.

Commenting on nineteenth-century American representations of Italian life, William Vance argues that due recognition should be given to

their democratic quality. By choosing quotidian scenes and common
humanity as their privileged subject, picturesque art and literature "not
only responded to democratic taste but constituted a democratic affirma-
tion"; they found "the people worthy of serious treatment." He also
notes, however, that the initial democratic impulse often gave way to a
drastically different ideological approach.

> The traits that make people "picturesque," however "real," are their pecu-
> liarities of dress and custom.... These differences, rather than a common
> humanity, easily became the primary purpose of representation. And the
> appreciation for "quaint" and "colorful" superficialities, rather than typical
> human qualities and universal conditions, commonly encouraged a conde-
> scending attitude in cultivated readers and patrons. (1990, 2:142)

The desire to document another people's way of life and traditions
may come, as we have seen, from an exclusive concern with that
society's past. When such is the case, it is assumed that change invariably comports an irredeemable loss. As regards the field of this study,
one finds books in which the amelioration of deplorable living conditions
in certain parts of Italy is forcefully advocated on the (paradoxical)
condition that things remain essentially as they are.

Coming from a land whose rhythm of life seemed frantic, especially if
compared to that of southern Europe, and where looking back in time
might be regarded as unproductive, many Americans witnessed Italy's
historical evolution with mixed emotions. To them, Italy's technological
backwardness appeared at once melancholy and appealing. Similarly, the
tremendous advance of modernity in the United States might be viewed
as bringing benefits or enveloping the nation with a gloomy hue of grey.
And if the second, pessimistic view prevailed, Italy assumed the fantastic
connotation of a place where one might still recover what the irresistible
march of technology obliterated in its way. To be sure, the step from
such a characterization to that of "home of the past" was but a short one.

To those with a retrospective turn of mind, the land anciently known
by the name Hesperia offered abundant reasons for reflection, with its
rich variety of historical layers. In this sense, it is well to note, as I. M.
Battafarano has done in a paper on Viktor Hehn,[2] that the foreign colony
in Italy was not composed exclusively of painters, sculptors, writers, and
simple tourists, but also of a good number of geologists and naturalists.

To these environmental investigators, Italy seemed a land where "the traces of the history of the earth" were preserved better than in other countries, and not only "in the morphology of the territory" but also in "plants and rocks" (1989, 131). They saw Italy as a land literally imbued with history.

One wonders what sort of impact this pervasive sense of the past could have had on the representatives of such a young culture as that of white Northern America. What is certain is that the Italian reader of American travel books must make a special effort in order to relate to their views of the past. Most of us, and I am speaking as an Italian, in fact grow up and live day after day in such familiarity with buildings, statues, and all sorts of vestiges from remote epochs that to our eyes they often blend with the landscape. They are part of our quotidian experience; to put it simply, they are just there. This is not to say that Italians do not look back at their past; indeed, looking back is one of the few things that may be said to unite Milan and Rome, Venice and Naples, the North and the South. The Italian who is born and lives in a city or region that has had a period of supremacy in politics or the arts, or both, is usually well aware of that past, and this seems to be true at all social and cultural levels. It is a past in which people recognize themselves, a past not regarded as a closed chapter but rather as an integral part of one's heritage, as something that has a role to play in the shaping of one's life. What needs to be emphasized, though, is that such a past, no matter how fondly remembered, is not a rigidly defined concept but an exquisitely vague mental construct. It is a loosely demarcated yesterday whose distance from today — whatever number of centuries it may span — is experienced as neither intimidating nor distressing. One takes it for granted, as part of the order of things. It is an attitude toward time and its visible marks, which, as we shall see in the chapter on *The Marble Faun*, is in clear contrast with that of Hawthorne.

The variety of cultural individualities of cities and regions was not a prominent theme in most nineteenth-century American books on Italy, and this despite the fact that the differences that separated and distinguished each urban nucleus or area were emphasized, before the 1860–70 decade, by the presence of concrete and inescapable signs of division. How could travelers not confront the political and legislative separation between the various Italian states when, to traverse even relatively short tracts of territory, they had to pass through customs and exhibit their passports? (Complaints about this not insignificant inconvenience recur in practically every single account of a journey through Italy.)

For an author who intended to establish a comparison with the United States, it was surely more feasible to think of Italy as a compact cultural entity than as a mosaic of localisms. Generalizations — both positive and negative — were common. Those of the negative type possibly indicated a need to propagandize an American model of society. Summing up Italy as a country dominated by despotism, superstition, and indigence could be useful, for such a portrayal emphasized by contrast the ambitions of the United States, the most aggressive of emerging cultures. Italy could serve as a reminder of what the founding fathers had meant to leave behind them on their way to the New World. A broad characterization was far more effective, in this sense, than a detailed description. The insufficient acquaintance with the Italian language paradoxically became an advantage, as to the locals could be ascribed all sorts of words and intentions. The fact that social contact was limited to brief, purely functional exchanges (as with servants, coachmen, hotel-keepers) gave one greater freedom to invent, to supply with one's imagination what could not come through experience. Undoubtedly though, this approach might serve equally well the opposite generalization. What was only superficially observed might be more easily romanticized. What was seen through the filter of fondly remembered descriptions and illustrations was likely to be idealized. Thus it happened that the Italian rural landscape was viewed as possessing an oneiric, visionary quality, and the people who inhabited it — peasants, laborers, etc. — were believed to have stepped out of the pages of a pastoral poem, or a painting, or thought to be statues who had magically abandoned the coldness of marble for the warmth of flesh and blood.

Americans in Italy were themselves the subject of constructions that were often all the more fanciful because they were based exclusively on extremely vague information. Throughout Italy, notions about the United States were mostly dim or extravagant, and not merely among the lower and middle classes but also among the nobility and even, sometimes, the heads of state. What is more, for a surprisingly large number of people, America was a non-entity. Its citizens were commonly called "inglesi" [English], a frequent cause of irritation for many U. S. travelers and an actual disadvantage: among all foreign visitors of Italy, the least popular were precisely those from England.

For those Italians who were aware of the country's existence, the name "America" could bring to mind two completely different pictures, depending on the quality of their information and their sensibility. The first was that of a land untouched by Western civilization and where nature reigned sovereign. The presence of a population of European descent did not fit this picture, and the inhabitants of this fabulous country could only be dark-skinned "savages." Not surprisingly then, the fair complexion of American travelers frequently caused surprise, as did their dress, devoid as it was of colorful feathers.

There is more to this notion of America than a simple removal of an entire historical phase (white colonization). One discovers in fact at its core an idea that was deeply rooted in the Italian collective imagination: the idea that foreigners were all, more or less, uncivilized (something that has not completely disappeared and that in our time finds expression in the media's treatment of the phenomenon of mass tourism: words such as "hordes" and "invasion" are common, as is the label of "new barbarians" applied to the numerous foreign visitors of Florence, Rome, Venice, and other art cities). The reality of Italy's diminished standing in the world was challenged through a vindication of its heritage, while the achievements of others were ignored or devalued. As Giulio Bollati justly points out, this attitude only demonstrated that what Italy had certainly inherited from classical civilization was its radical ethnocentrism. Significantly, he notes, the belief in the privileges deriving from classical descent, and the conviction of being an expression of the "central nucleus of 'civilization'" were not shaken but rather reinforced by the reality of decadence. The "immensity of the fall" only emphasized the height; the "vastness of the damage" was viewed as "a sign of election and the legitimation of pride." In the coexistence of "supremacy and decadence, of objective inferiority," more than compensated through "an unconquered sense of superiority," Bollati finds "one of the most characteristic and stable patterns of the entire Italian history" (1989, 956).

The other popular image of America was that of a young, progressive, and prosperous nation. Its appeal was enormous, its connotation mythical. To those who hoped that Italy might be made one and independent, and who believed in the free circulation of ideas, the United States represented the ultimate symbol of democracy. It was the country in which they saw realized that project of liberty whose possibilities of success in Italy seemed so remote. According to this view, the United States had not changed since 1776, and the country still rigorously abided by the values expressed in its constitution. As Giuseppe Prezzolini pointed out, many Italians thought of the American people chiefly as responsible for "a liberal revolution," and they did not realize that what was gradually emerging from that beginning was an empire (1971, 19–20). Doubtlessly, most Americans in Italy were intensely aware of the particular reputation and emblematic quality of their government, and this might have colored their interpretation of the historical moment both in the United States and in Italy.

The role of the landscape — fundamental in most literary genres — assumes a particular complexity in texts in which the scene described is unfamiliar to the author. What needs to be taken into account is not merely how the landscape reveals itself to the author's perception, how it is emotionally apprehended, but also how the author's notions of culture affect his or her reactions. The interpretation of a new landscape is made difficult by the absence of recognizable reference marks, of signs — chromatic, auditory, etc. — that are part of our experience and memory. In their place one finds other elements that tell of a different culture, a different relation between man and space, a different use of the territory. Hence the occurrence of what Eugenio Turri has described as a state of "psychological uneasiness," a sense of disquiet similar to that provoked by an obscure language or by different customs. What we react to is, in his words, "the foreign country, humanized by a different culture in a different environmental background, [a culture] that uses and feels the landscape in a different way, even though on the basis of natural functions identical to ours" (1983, 140).

It is relevant to the study of travel literature, then, to determine whether an author is able to overcome that initial uneasiness, whether his or her work reveals — to use Turri's expression — "a capacity to sense … the innermost relations between man and environment." For to understand the signs of the landscape means "to go beyond them and to relate them structurally to the other manifestations of a culture" (1983, 141).

In the period with which this study is concerned, Italy's condition of political division and subjugation had a paralyzing influence on the country's economic and social evolution. At the same time, though, these factors favored the persistence of a preindustrial relation between man and nature. As a consequence, the Italian landscape still maintained many of those traits that had reached their highest expression with the Renaissance. Wandering through the country, especially its central regions, the traveler could still find areas in which the same artistic principle seemed to inform, without apparent interruption, houses and fields, palaces and hills, churches and groves. Instead of the traumatic scenic alteration that was taking place in the most industrialized countries, Italy offered examples of a harmonious interrelation between architecture and environment (Turri 1979, 155). In contrast to the threat of cultural homogenization that seemed to accompany technological advance, the Italian territory presented a wide variety of forms and colors. And the country's many and different landscapes exemplified distinct local uses of space, original ways of inserting urban structures in natural settings.

If this multiplicity was primarily a source of interest, curiosity, or aesthetic pleasure, its preservation through the centuries could also suggest a reflection on the character of time, on the pace of life. There were, as we have seen, American artists who worried about the survival of certain aspects of Italian life under the pressure of modernity, and strove to "save" them from disappearance by describing them in their works. But there were also many of their colleagues and fellow country-men who envisioned Italy as a country not regulated by ordinary tempo-ral laws. For them, Italy represented a refuge from the incessant motion of history. An American might find solace in the near immobility of the Italian scene, where attention to the single passing moment took the place of a race for achievement which dramatically emphasized one's mortality.

The idea that the country's pace of life was so slow that it might be almost mistaken for a stasis circulated also among certain Italian intellec-tual circles, although with different connotations. What was described by others as "serenity" and "tranquillity" became "paralysis" or "lethargy" in the writings of some of the Italian romantics. The readers were contin-uously exhorted to awaken from their "slumber," and that call had a clear political implication: to awaken meant to claim one's rights and to free the country from the foreign forces that kept it divided.

The Italian sojourn of an American writer, like that of his European counterparts, was not generally characterized by any significant relation-ship with the local population. Cases like that of Fuller's marriage with the Marquis Giovanni Angelo Ossoli and Howells's friendship with Eugenio Brunetta constitute exceptions rather than the norm, a norm made mostly of the kind of brief, ordinary encounters with the low orders of society to which the traveler was necessarily exposed in his trips from city to city. If differences in usages and mores, as well as the language barrier, certainly represented a considerable difficulty, so did the social gulf that separated travelers from locals. The sense of disorientation affecting visitors resulted not only, I believe, from the foreignness of the scene, but also from the fact that, outside Anglo-American circles, their only social contact was with people who were not their social peers. They had to deal with men and women who were, one might say, doubly foreign: in both culture and class.

Another element to consider is the presence in Italy in the years under consideration of an underclass of beggars and paupers which for its mass and diffusion had no equivalent in the United States. This presence was so obsessive that it is almost safe to say that no journal of travel through Italy fails to comment on it. These people, not only of miserable appearance but also frequently disfigured or maimed, very likely offered a disheartening spectacle, not to mention a constant source of irritation, with their insistent requests for alms. Children, in particular, would follow the foreign visitor to their city or village literally step by step, thus superimposing the unpleasantness of their poverty onto suggestive backgrounds of churches and monuments. Writing on the 1860 Italian journey of the German writer Karl Hillebrand, Lucia Borghese maintains that, in reacting with a sense of repugnance to the spectacle of misery, the bourgeoisie reveals its "bad social conscience." When poverty is not meek and subdued but aggressive, Borghese explains, it assumes the upsetting character of an "economic claim" made by the victims of exploitation (1987, 55–56). For Americans, the impact of the inescapable evidence of want and destitution in Italy was proportional to the contrast with the reality they had left behind. As citizens of a realized democracy, they could find in what they saw both a confirmation of the fairness of their social system and a warning of what might happen if its original principles were abandoned.

In Hans Christian Andersen's 1835 novel *The Improvisatore* — a highly influential work for the literary representation of Italy — there is an episode that effectively illustrates the common Protestant view of Roman Catholic worship. In chapter 6, Antonio (the protagonist of the story) and Domenica (the peasant woman who takes care of him after the death of his mother) are seen ascending the steps of the Borghese palace in Rome. On their way, they pass beautiful statues standing in niches.

One of these marble figures attracts Domenica's attention; she stops, kneels before it, and crosses herself. But that statue, the hero/narrator informs us, is not what Domenica takes it to be: it is not the Madonna, but rather the Roman goddess Vesta. What is suggested is, of course, the link, the continuity between paganism and Catholicism, the idea that at the basis of the Roman Catholic Church there is a simple disguise or adaptation of heathen customs. In addition, Andersen here touches on the relationship between religion and art in Italy, something at once fascinating and disturbing for most Protestants. The origin of Domenica's mistake, in fact, is to be traced back to a philosophy of art that privileges the representation of beauty. Indeed, it may be difficult for the uninformed to distinguish between statues (or pictures) of Vesta and other pagan goddesses and those of the Madonna. As subjects, the episode seems to suggest, they are treated by Italian artists with equal reverence and devotion in that they all inspire the portrayal of noble and beautiful features.

A Protestant's response to religion in Italy was (and still is, though to a lesser degree) very likely to be subtly interwoven with his or her experience of the great art of the past. One could, for instance, compare the limpid piety and austerity of the early masters (such as Giotto or Fra Angelico) — expression of the original integrity of Catholicism — with the reality of temporal despotism, corruption, and worldliness of nineteenth-century Rome. Or, if one believed the Catholic faith to have been hopelessly tainted from the start, because based on false principles and superstitions, there remained the question of reconciling this conviction with the presence of art works that found their source and themes in that creed. The evaluation of Italian art could hardly be, in most cases, the result of merely aesthetic considerations. What needs to be considered, then, is not only the way in which this art is described and appreciated by a Protestant observer, but also his or her awareness (or lack of it) of the particular difficulties involved in the matter. We should try to see, in other words, whether such an individual relies confidently and exclusively on his or her criteria, or approaches the subject acknowledging the need for careful study and interpretation.

Finally, it is well to remember that by traveling to Italy in the nineteenth century, the American writer, painter, or sculptor joined an international community of artists that had found in the Mediterranean peninsula its most congenial environment. The impression of its simultaneous presence added to that of the visible traces of the work of former masters and easily induced thoughts on the possibilities of art in different lands and different times. The many travel journals, novels, stories, and poems on Italy by American authors were often inspired by such reflections. More or less openly, then, their readers were invited to muse on the role of the artist in America, on whether the choices that the country was making would render it central or marginal.

# Backward Glances

# 1

## Italy as the "Land of Opportunities": Margaret Fuller's Travel Letters for *The New York Tribune* (1847–49) and Julia Ward Howe's *Passion Flowers* (1854)

Margaret Fuller's letters from Italy for *The New York Tribune* cover a period rich in political ferment all over Europe, culminating in the national uprisings of 1848. In particular, as a correspondent in Rome, she had the opportunity to record firsthand for her American readers the dramatic events that led to the rise and fall of the short-lived Roman Republic (February-July 1849) and to the French occupation of the city. She witnessed and commented on the introduction of cautious, tentative reforms by Pope Pius IX; his subsequent dissociation from the nationalistic movement; his flight from Rome; the proclamation of the republic; the brief but tenacious resistance of the republican forces against the French army (sent by Louis Napoleon to restore papal sovereignty); the siege and final capitulation of Rome.

Equally tumultuous were the events directly affecting her private life. Toward the end of 1847, at the age of thirty-seven, Fuller found herself pregnant and unmarried. After a difficult pregnancy, characterized by both physical and mental dejection, she gave birth to a son in the little town of Rieti on 5 September 1848. The father was a young nobleman, the Marquis Giovanni Angelo Ossoli, whom Fuller probably married in the course of the same year (it is not known whether this happened before or after the child's birth, as no official record of the ceremony has ever been found). What is certain is that both maternity and marriage were kept secret for a long time. Fuller feared the hostile reactions of acquaintances and colleagues at home because of the irregularity of the relationship and the fact that Ossoli was nine years younger than she, a Catholic, an aristocrat, and certainly not an intellectual.[1] Ossoli was not less apprehensive about the attitude of his family: their close ties with the papal government could not make them regard with favor a connection with a Protestant, especially one with "subversive" ideas. Because of their involvement in the "adventure" of the republic (the marquis fought in the ranks of the Republican Army), the Ossolis had no choice but to abandon Rome when it fell into the hands of the French.

It was that sad city, patrolled by foreign troops, that was portrayed, a few years later, in Julia Ward Howe's *Passion Flowers* (1854). Howe's lyrical response to Italy or, more specifically, to Rome, is to be traced back to her stay there between the fall of 1850 and the spring of 1851. It was her second trip to Italy, as she had previously traveled through the country in the winter of 1843–44 (in the course of a European tour that had begun a week after her marriage). On that occasion she had met Count Confalonieri (one of the most prominent Italian patriots of the time and a former prisoner at Spielberg) and the Marchioness Costanza Arconati Visconti (a strong supporter of the moderate party[2] and, later, a good friend of Margaret Fuller), and had been received by Pope Gregory XVII.

The scene that presented itself to Howe's observation during the 1850–51 sojourn was apparently similar to that of her earlier trip. At that time, the domination of both foreign and local tyrannies had seemed to Howe complete. But the country in which she returned in 1850 had lived through the nationalistic enthusiasm of 1848–49, and Rome had seen the unthinkable: the end (however temporary) of the political power of the pope.

The chronological proximity of Fuller and Howe's Roman sojourns is only one of the many links between the two writers. In her 1982 biography of Howe, Mary H. Grant points out that the author of *Passion Flowers* "wished intensely to emulate Fuller's literary success." Indeed, such was Howe's interest in Fuller's life and works that she wrote Fuller's biography (1883) and edited a collection of her letters (1903). Fuller, Grant further observes, "had led the way to Rome" for many American intellectual women, and Howe "must have seen the parallels" (1982, 190) between their two experiences. She must have noted, in particular, that in both instances the sojourn abroad coincided with the upset of one's established image and role. As had been the case with Fuller, the Roman experience assumed for Howe the character of a turning point. Howe's husband,[3] who, in their first seven years of marriage, had consistently limited her nondomestic interests and activities, chose not to follow her to Italy in 1850. His absence gave Howe a long-awaited opportunity to act exclusively according to her own judgment, an opportunity that would eventually lead to her debut as a writer. *Passion Flowers* was Howe's first published book, and it had great success. Doubtlessly, its popularity owed much to the uninhibited, passionate tone of the poems and their "daring" exposition of a Boston lady's emotional life (the author's identity, initially protected by anonymity, was very soon discovered). But *Passion Flowers* was also critically acclaimed and received praise from such eminent figures as Henry Wadsworth Longfellow, John G. Whittier, Ralph Waldo Emerson, and Theodore Parker.

The image of Italy that emerges most distinctly from the works considered in this chapter is that of a territory to be explored. The discovery and the conquest of this new frontier possesses the irresistible charm of transgression; it promises the "hidden wealth of untried potentialities" (to use Remotti's expression [1990, 47]). Furthermore, I use the word "conquest" in relation to Fuller and Howe's writings because in them the acts of observing and describing are a form of appropriation of the experience. In contrast to the reassuring sense of detachment that most representations of foreign countries tend to communicate to the reader, Fuller and Howe's attitudes are those of intense involvement with the object of their attention. Both express a desire to participate and are willing to compromise, to endanger their privileged point of view; their attitude is the antithesis, for example, of that "emotional calm" which Vincent Crapanzano (1986, 62) has described as informing Goethe's *Italian Journey* (1789).

The sense of interaction with historical reality that is conveyed by some of the poems of *Passion Flowers* may be fully appreciated if we compare them to Howe's reflections on her first Italian visit. At that time, Rome had struck her as "something seen in a dream" and had charmed her with its "gloom" and "silence." Still, she had been unfavorably impressed by what she regarded as excessive formality and ceremony in the city's social life. Like other travelers, she had found amusement "for a time" in "the strangeness of titles, the glitter of jewels," but the return to America had seemed to her a return to "the living world" (1899, 122, 127, 133). Inevitably, by 1850 her view was different. She was confronted with the prospect of uncontrolled social and intellectual experimentation. This first chance for independence resulted in a complete reversal of her former views. Rome, and Italy by extension, began in fact to be associated with the idea of unhampered movement and expression, while home gradually came to stand for stifling rigidity of manners and feelings. The opening of the long poem entitled "Rome" well exemplifies this contrast. A walk through the city becomes the means of renouncing and denying the values of domestic rigor, of purpose and duty, and of reclaiming one's individuality and the capacity for sensory apprehension. It is the fruition of reality in its entirety (nature, art, the past, the present, etc.) that overwhelms any constriction (the heart's "sadly cherished silence" and "long sealed tides") and finds its voice in one's "wild singing" (8–9).[4] The city becomes, in Howe's representation, a new terrain that the reader is invited to penetrate and discover. And the landscape is experienced as a mass of scattered pieces being collected and accumulated, almost greedily.

> I strayed, amassing wild flowers, ivy leaves,
> Relics, and crusted marbles, gathering too
> Thoughts of unending Beauty from the fields (8)

Returning to Fuller and the idea of Italy as a territory to be explored, it is possible to detect a connection between her dispatches for *The New York Tribune* and an earlier work that she devoted to a rather different subject: *Summer on the Lakes, in 1843* (1844). In this book Fuller describes the life and possibilities of Midwest settlers whom she had the chance to observe and meet in the course of a tour of Illinois and the Wisconsin Territory. Traveling for the first time out of her native New England, Fuller found herself, almost to her surprise, strongly captivated by the vastness and beauty of the new environment. The prairies struck her as a sort of ideal garden, rich with the promises of a new beginning, a new Eden waiting to be populated. Gradually though, something emerged from her contacts and interviews with the settlers that dimmed that idyllic picture. She became aware that the enjoyment of that magnificent garden was almost completely denied to women.[5] Even in that realm of openness, women found themselves imprisoned within a narrow space: the four walls of a roughly built cabin. What's more, if the drudgery of housework, augmented by all sorts of discomforts, kept them confined for most of the day, the lack of any useful, practical element in their education made the enjoyment of nature on their part highly improbable (1991, 38–39).

Something of Fuller's initial rapture at the sight of the seemingly boundless prairies, something of her enthusiasm at the prospect of new possibilities, reappears, I believe, in her letters from Italy. Fuller views Italy, in a sense, as a new domain that she can make her own. Like the prairie in *Summer on the Lakes*, Italy appears to her a "field of possibilities," and one even further removed from the limitations and conventions of her original background. Hence we find in her letters a repeatedly expressed aspiration to be a part of the scene, a scene made of people to meet, places to explore, and historical incidents of great import. It is an aspiration which, if fulfilled, results in a passage from "'talk to life,' from contemplation to commitment, from sentimental experience to sustained action" (Salomone 1968, 1378).

If most American artists who resided in Italy were delighted to discover that their profession was well regarded within the local culture, the women among them found additional satisfaction in the fact that as painters, sculptors, or writers, they were allowed greater social freedom than at home. The often rigid social and behavioral codes of their communities could not apply to the cosmopolitan intellectual circles of Rome, where nonconformity and even eccentricity were easily accepted. The special appeal that Rome could have for women artists did not escape Nathaniel Hawthorne's attention; he effectively captured it both in his journal (as, for instance, in the portrayal of the sculptress Harriet Hosmer) and in *The Marble Faun*. For Hawthorne's heroines Hilda and Miriam, Rome represents a unique opportunity for free conduct and association, for unprecedented independence. In chapter 6 of *The Marble Faun*, the narrator tells us that Hilda "was an example of the freedom of life which it is possible for a female artist to enjoy at Rome." Later on in the book, commenting on the mystery surrounding Miriam's origins, the sculptor Kenyon remarks that "nowhere else but in Rome, and as an artist, could she hold a place in society without giving some clue to her past life" (1986, 54, 109).

How the possibility of experiencing such liberty might color a woman artist's emotional response to the city is amply demonstrated by the sense of exhilaration conveyed by many passages in Fuller's letters and Howe's poems. Whether the emphasis is mostly on place (as in Howe) or on people (as in Fuller), both authors seem particularly alert to capture the sheer energy of life. When Howe, for instance, contemplates the city at dusk, with its "mystical shapes, that deepened into joy" (9), or Fuller, visiting the cemetery of Santo Spirito, meditates on the tombs "in which once dwelt joyous Roman hearts — for the hearts here do take pleasure in life" (260),[6] the impression is one of emotional awakening. As with Hilda's comings and goings in *The Marble Faun*, the reader following the wanderings of Fuller and Howe cannot but become aware of the sense of ease and naturalness of movement that characterize such moments. Yet, whereas Hawthorne's New England copyist walks through the city with her feet barely touching the ground (such is the author's concern that her purity be isolated from the filth around her), Fuller and Howe never remain aloof, and consistently search for contact with whatever scene presents itself to them.

Their representation of Italy corresponds, then, to an exploration, an adventurous journey. And yet their course, however direct, tends to lead them back to their starting point: America. The deeper they penetrate the unknown territory, the clearer becomes their view of home. In the process, their privileged interlocutor and travel companion, the American reader, is encouraged to question and redefine his or her cultural identity.

Commenting on Fuller's passionate commitment to the fate of the Roman Republic of 1849, Rosella Mamoli Zorzi justly observes that if, on the one hand, this New England writer increasingly identifies with the city, on the other, she never "ceases to relate her experience" to America; indeed she even "intensifies ... her 'Americanness'" (1986, xiii). Within Fuller's analysis of the historical moment in Italy, America is repeatedly, insistently adduced. The transition from the Italian to the American scene in the letters is always swift and effortless, almost automatic, as if the struggle for democracy at any level, in any country, were to Fuller's eyes but a rehearsal of the birth of her nation. She regards as culpable all those who show little or no concern for what is at stake in Italy. In her opinion, however, Americans are more to be blamed, for they fail to recognize what, in spite of differences in culture and circumstances, is the same animating principle that was at the basis of America's own revolution. A scant self-knowledge, Fuller seems to suggest, prevents the identification of the image in the mirror of history.

They [the Americans] have no heart for the idea, for the destiny of our own great nation: how can they feel the spirit that is struggling in this and others of Europe? (240)

For Fuller, the idea, the destiny of America is clearly its role as preserver and promoter of liberty. It is a role the nation has taken upon itself since its creation, and that finds expression in the original Declaration of Independence of 1776. In order to remain true to the nature of that document, America has the duty to use its prosperity and growing political influence to oppose tyranny in the Old World: "The cause is OURS, above all others.... Ah! America, with all thy rich boons, thou hast a heavy account to render for the talent given" (249). Such appeals occur in several letters, their tone becoming increasingly emphatic as Fuller shares more and more intensely in the dramatic events taking place in Rome and the rest of Italy. The experience of Italy, as Bell Gale Chevigny writes in *The Woman and the Myth*, clarifies for Fuller "the source of her frustrations with America in her time" (1976, 375). When she invokes what she sees as America's sacred mission, she also reminds her country of how it has already, on more than one occasion, betrayed its calling. In Fuller's view, the Declaration of Independence ("which, if fully interpreted and acted upon, leaves nothing to be desired" [1971 (1856), 254]), or, one might say, the entire ethical heritage of the founding fathers of the nation, is denied by the "cancer of slavery" (255), the "boundless lust of gain" (254), and the war against Mexico. Thus, Fuller observes, instead of the contrast that there ought to be between the situation in the New World and in Europe, one is confronted with the shameful symmetry with which injustice is committed in both continents.

> I listen to the same arguments against the emancipation of Italy, that are used against the emancipation of our blacks; the same arguments in favor of the spoliation of Poland, as for the conquest of Mexico. I find the cause of tyranny and wrong everywhere the same, — and lo! my country! ... no champion of the rights of men, but a robber and a jailer. (255)

From her new vantage point, Fuller is now able to reconsider and appreciate the efforts of the abolitionists, who, at home, seemed to her "tedious," "narrow," "rabid," and "exaggerated" (255), and to stigmatize with lucidity what she regards as America's removal from its democratic beginnings: the metamorphosis of the eagle, originally and ideally the emblem of liberty, into a bird of prey (254). Looming in the near future, she seems to suggest, is the possibility that those beginnings become simply an empty myth, a possibility that appears to find expression in the complacency of some of her countrymen. It is to them that Fuller's appeals are addressed with particular fervor, for a little effort on their part to become better acquainted with the political turmoil of Europe would inevitably bring them to question the state of democracy in their country. The study of the European scene would make them realize the imminence and inevitability of a new phase in the evolution of modern democracies, the recognition as the "aristocracy of nations" of "the LABORING CLASSES" (306).

It is Fuller's particular concern, throughout her twenty-one dispatches that her readers live as fully as possible the predicament of the Italian people, the oppression of tyrannical governments, and the enthusiasm for the first steps toward liberty, in order to be continuously reminded of the inestimable value they are jeopardizing. For this reason she inserts in her letters translations of official and political documents (often in their entirety), such as Giuseppe Mazzini's letter to Pope Pius IX[7] (8 September 1847, 284–91) or the pope's advice of excommunication[8] (6 January 1849, 351–53). Although Fuller's pessimism about the moral health of her country seems to increase with the passing of months, her criticism, however pungent, is never unaccompanied by the expression of hope for change, for the chance that America will finally assume leadership of the international democratic movement. The expectation of such an event seems almost to take on, at some point, the character of a crucial condition for Fuller's return. The spirit that has made America "all it is of value" to her is "more alive" (326) in Europe, where

> amid the teachings of adversity, a nobler spirit is struggling, — a spirit which cheers and animates mine. I hear earnest words of pure faith and love. I see deeds of brotherhood. This is what makes *my* America. I do not deeply distrust my country. She is not dead, but in my time she sleepeth, and the spirit of our fathers flames no more, but lies hid beneath the ashes. (327)

What ultimately prevents Fuller from distrusting her country is an unwavering belief in the uniqueness of its origins, that "pattern of spotless worth" (373) that sets America apart from all other nations, both as regards privileges and duties.

If, accepting Geertz's definition, we conceive of culture as an "acted document" (1973, 10), we might say that the underlying suggestion in Howe's *Passion Flowers* too is that the document be interpreted in its entirety. The experience of Italy in the mid-nineteenth century cannot possibly exclude, in her view, the country's political situation. Sightseeing or the study of art alone have little meaning; to select only certain aspects (what is pleasant or picturesque, for instance) of Italian reality is tantamount to limiting one's attention to the illustrations of a book while ignoring the text. Like Fuller, Howe directs her harshest criticism against the self-satisfaction of some of her compatriots, expression of a deaf isolationism that must be repudiated. Thus, in "From Newport to Rome," Howe unmasks the imperturbability, social grace, and prosperity of certain New England circles as utterly artificial and shallow. Newport is evoked in this poem as the realm of repression and stillness, a world of exquisite civility that firmly defends itself from any potential threat to its calm and uneventfulness.

> No earnest feeling passes you
> Without dilution infinite;
> No word with frank abruptness breathed
> Must vent itself on ears polite. (60)

Reserve, tact, and elegance, Howe suggests, are but well-disguised and refined forms of deception, and tranquillity is preserved through an egotistical separation from the turmoils, pains, and passions of the rest of the world ("oh! do you hear that woeful strain" [61]). Without such a separation, that life would be stripped of its illusory brilliance and revealed in all its futility and emptiness ("Before those lurid bursts of flame / Your clustering wax-lights flicker pale" [63]).

Leaving behind us the cold composure of Newport, we are led, in the central part of the poem, through the explosion of sound, color, and movement that took place in Rome during the 1849 siege. Softly spoken words are succeeded by "thick and hurried speech" (62), the graceful figures of a dance by the disordered movement of fighters and casualties, the delicate hues and glitter of jewels and dresses by the vividness of smoke and blood.

A contrasting imagery characterizes the first section (40–41) of "A Protest from Italy," America being presented as a land traversed by clamor and contention, and Italy as one of calm and peace. Yet, in contrast with "From Newport to Rome," tumult and animation are not equated with vitality but rather regarded with annoyance. The fierce dispute over slavery, as heard from afar, almost suggests a childish prattle ("I sighed: 'Hush! hush! my countrymen / Let this untempered babbling cease!" [41]), as if the country had still a certain crudeness, a certain immaturity in its nature. One should notice, however, that while chastising the incoherent, excited tone of the debate, Howe is far from denigrating the importance of the problem, as its treatment in this and other poems (particularly "The Death of the Slave Lewis," 160–64) amply demonstrates.

Opposed to the confused sound of overlapping voices from America are the serenity and silence Howe sees as reigning over the Italian landscape and creating an atmosphere that bespeaks wisdom. Her words here recall Fuller's in a letter written at the close of the tumultuous year 1848. "The temper of life [in Rome] is repose," Fuller observes, and no matter how intense one's participation in the present, the inescapable influence of the past reduces all things, including "the emotions of the moments" (336), to their true proportions. The recognition of this phenomenon as an integral part of the experience of Rome is also at the core of Howe's depiction of the city in "A Protest from Italy."

The harsh sounds coming from America disrupt only temporarily the predominant calm, and the close of this section of the poem, with its references to inebriation and sleep, characterizes the contrast between the two countries as one between reality and dream. The second section confirms the impression, representing the change of vantage point from Italy to America as an abrupt awakening. Once again we are confronted with opposites conveyed through sensory expressions: hard ("sharp steel wind") versus soft ("silken armor"), noise ("trumpet's brazen voice") versus music ("mass and anthem") (42). As a result of the new perspective, however, the look of things is altered. However unpleasant, the confusion and roughness of the American scene are now viewed as possessing an invigorating quality ("My blood its natural current makes" [43]) — a quality that now invests Howe's vision and characterizes her concern for questions that earlier she had dismissed. With accents that recall Fuller's, Howe tells of a country where justice is declining and materialism is on the rise.

> Back, baleful force! back, perjured law!
> Sacred while ye the right sustain,

> But fallen like Judas, to betray
> The sinless blood for love of gain. (43)

It is a harsh indictment of slavery, a "plague" (42) doubly hateful not only because it cancels man's fundamental rights but because it originates from greed. The evocation of the figure of Judas seems to suggest that for Howe, as for Fuller, America's betrayal of the principle of liberty is a betrayal of a God-determined design. Yet, while denouncing America's desertion of the cause of righteousness, she indirectly reasserts, through the emphatic quality of her expressions, her ties with her native land. Although voicing her emotional estrangement from the moral climate of the country in the final section ("The natural loves that move my heart, / My country, matter not to thee" [44]), Howe at the same time shows that it is toward America that her gaze is most intensely and frequently directed.

> however dear
> I hold the light of Roman skies;
> However from the canvas clear
> The soul of Raphael blessed mine eyes;
>
> Howe'er intense the joy of flowers,
> And the spring-wedded nightingale,
> Or deep the charm of twilight hours
> Hushed to the Miserère's wail;
> A holier joy to me were given,
> Could I persuade thy heart from wrong; (45)

As in the nineteenth century, present-day travel books offer the reader recommendations on what is worth seeing in a foreign country. Less numerous, however, are the works that concentrate on the difficult and delicate question of how things should be seen. Fuller's letters (beside their obvious historical value) have the added attraction of being able to be considered a sort of treatise on travel. They contain in fact the methodology of that "exploration" of the Italian territory to which I referred earlier. "At Genoa and Leghorn, I saw for the first time Italians in their homes" (218), Fuller announces in the very first of her reports for *The Tribune*, a statement that sets the tone of her research. The dwellings of ordinary people are as worthy of interest, in Fuller's analysis, as the imposing edifices designed by celebrated artists, for they are all expressions of the same culture. They tell, albeit in different ways, of local uses of space, of local ideas of beauty and utility. It is not too surprising then, to discover that one of the buildings most effectively and affectingly described in the letters is a private abode: a "clean, simple house" near St. Peter's.

> It bore on a tablet that it was the property of Angela — ; its little balconies with their old wooden rails, full of flowers in humble earthen vases, the many bird-cages, the air of domestic quiet and comfort, marked it as the home of some vestal or widow, some lone woman whose heart was centred in the ordinary and simplest pleasures of a home. (399)

The house is not seen here simply as a building, as an architectural artifact, but as the expression of "a view of the world" (Turri 1983, 218). As Fuller's careful choice of terms indicates, Angela's dwelling represents an ideal of calm, purity, and decorum. However, the significance of such a modest little piece of reality is very likely to escape altogether the "traveller pressing along the beaten track" (220), equally ignorant of the language of the buildings as of that of their builders. For Fuller, not much can be learned about a country or a people when there is no emotional sharing in what meets one's gaze. An authentic knowledge of Italy may only come, in her words, through "an intimacy of feeling, an abandonment to the spirit of the place" (220). To the distance that typical travelers put between themselves and the scene in front of them (a distance signaled by the "constant use of the pronoun 'that'" [262]), Fuller opposes the utmost identification. Hers is an unceasing effort to assume the other's subjectivity: for example, of a Catholic woman ("Ave Maria Santissima! ... Madonna Addolorata! ... O Stella!" [378–79]) or of a Roman patriot ("I was struck more than ever by the heroic valor of *our* people, — let me so call them now as ever" [420]).

In one of the early letters, Fuller explains her growing interest and enthusiasm for the cause of Italian independence as the natural result of careful, unprejudiced observation as well as of previously acquired familiarity with the history, language and literature of the country. Observation and knowledge, she maintains, can alter dramatically an American's experience of Europe and, consequently, understanding of America as well. Considering how much of what is part of America's reality can be traced back to the Old World, "the American in Europe, if a thinking mind, can only become more American" (250). For this individual, Europe is then, potentially, the theater of a quest that can lead to inestimable gains, that can illuminate "remote allusions and derivations," that can make one finally see "the pattern of the stuff, and understand the whole tapestry" (250).

I emphasize "potentially," however, because not all Americans are eager or willing to learn about themselves while learning about others. Some (the kind Fuller identifies as the "servile American" [250]), are only attracted to Europe's refinement and sophistication when these are expressed in their least valuable and most superficial form (titles, fashion, etc.). Such people form a class Fuller sees as fortunately doomed to extinction. Some (the kind she identifies as the "conceited American" [251]), convinced of being endowed with some sort of superiority, are too confident in their judgment to recognize that "some training, some devotion" are indispensable in order to grasp the full significance of the exquisite design and music of an "old Cremona violin," the "etiquettes of courts and camps," the "ritual of the Church," or "the legends which are the subject of pictures" and "the profound myths which are represented in the antique marbles" — the "result," in short, of many centuries in "the history of Humanity" (251). Yet their arrogance, their overconfidence, bespeaks a strong sense of independence that is certainly preferable to the languid decadence of the former category and that promises notable achievements if accompanied and refined by education. Finally there are others, described by Fuller as "thinking Americans," who are equally aware of America's privileges and potentialities and of the value of tradition. They are fervent students who do not "wish one seed from the past to be lost" (252), as it is their utmost aspiration that what they learn in the Old World be brought back and cultivated in the new one. And their cultural identity, Fuller strongly believes, is by no means obliterated by such efforts; it is, on the contrary, strengthened and enriched. Rather significantly, echoes of this view may be found in Fuller's observations on some of the American painters and sculptors she met in Rome and Florence. She approves of their presence in Italy, and reminds their critics at home that "American Art is not necessarily a reproduction of American Nature" (279), a concept later exemplified, as regards literature, by both Hawthorne and Henry James.

Like Fuller's letters, the "Italian" poems in *Passion Flowers* suggest a combination of the roles of observer and actor. The visitor of Rome in

1850, as imagined by Howe, is not provoked by the tranquillity and silence of the militarily occupied city to forget the events of the previous year. In contrast to the prevailing Protestant view of the pope as a sort of travel curiosity, Howe identifies with the voice of disappointed Italian nationalists in the explicitly political poem "Pio IX." It must be remembered that Pius IX's introduction of limited liberal reforms in the government of the papal state, in the late 1840s, had been greeted with enormous popular enthusiasm throughout Italy. Many had envisioned a unified Italian nation under the pope's leadership. Pius IX, however, dismayed at the ferments and expectations his reforms had encouraged, soon disclaimed any relation to the movement for self-government. In "Pio IX," the highest authority of the Roman Catholic Church is directly addressed and denounced for his lack of faith and courage. As seen by Howe, Pius IX's failure to live up to the role with which he had been identified is not merely a betrayal of popular hopes but an unpardonable act of resistance to divine purpose ("Thou should'st have trod the waters as a path, / Such power divine thy holy mission gave" [26]).

Both "From Newport to Rome" and "Whit-Sunday in the Church" confirm the impression that Howe's recreation of the images and voices of the Risorgimento functions at once as an appeal to the democratic conscience of her readers and a reminder that that part of reality cannot be excluded from a traveler's ken. The evocation of the 1849 siege in "From Newport to Rome" culminates in a denunciation of the French intervention that brought about the demise of the Roman Republic while other nations (first and foremost among which is of course, for Howe, America) remained culpably indifferent. The event is made to assume universal proportions and implications, as Howe, almost echoing the close of Fuller's last letter (1971 [1856], 421), reminds us of the "kinship of ... human blood" and the "high pangs of brotherhood" (1854, 66).

The same intensity and an equally firm conviction of the extraordinariness of the moment also animates "Whit-Sunday in the Church," in which liberty is celebrated as the ultimate Christian cause. Christ, as imagined by Howe, is a militant figure standing on the side of the oppressed and opposing all forms of despotism, including that of the church ("He stands where earnest minds assert / God's law against a creed dogmatic" [77]). His support is for the enslaved ("Where backs are scourged and limbs are corded" [76]), toiling peasants and workers, and political prisoners and activists, and his call is a call to arms.

'He cries: On, brethren! draw the sword;
Loose the bold tongue and pen, unfearing;
...
'Twas for the multitude I bled,
Not for the greatest, richest, whitest (77–78)

Reversing the trajectory of "From Newport to Rome," Howe moves here from the universal to the particular. In the last part of the poem, the "patriots" who "pine in cells" (77) are thus revealed to be prisoners at Spielberg ("those brave young Lombards dying" [78]), and Christ is consequently identified with the Italian nationalistic movement. The oppressed, mentioned earlier as an undistinguished mass, assume an individual, specific identity as "yonder negro babe" (78) torn away from its family. The fact that the two examples are placed one next to the other is of course hardly accidental. Like Fuller, Howe indicates in fact a parallel between the enslavement of Italians by foreign despots and the enslavement of blacks by whites in America. Another crucial point is explained in the last four stanzas. The earlier reference to Christ's dissociation from the church is expanded and clarified in his condemnation of the mundanity of Catholicism, its empty pomp and hypocritical priests.

Howe's extensive treatment of Italy's political vicissitudes does not appear to have influenced a large number of American writings on Italy. Interestingly enough, for example, an author like Hawthorne, who read with interest and reviewed (privately) *Passion Flowers*, almost completely avoided political references in delineating the Italian setting of *The Marble Faun*. In a series of letters to Boston publisher William D. Ticknor, Hawthorne expressed his mixed views of *Passion Flowers*. On the one hand, he strongly objected to the book's sentimental and autobiographical character, to what he regarded as a shameless display of innermost feelings, and went so far as to state that the author of the poems "ought to have been soundly whipt for publishing them." On the other hand, though, he found the poems "delightful" (1987, 18:53), "admirable" (17:177), and maintained that America had produced "no better poetry than some of her [Howe's] verses" (17:277). The last opinion is likely to have prevailed as regards the "Italian" poems, which may have represented a source for *The Marble Faun*, particularly as regards the recreation of the atmosphere of Rome.

In "Rome," the opening celebration of the city's beauty is followed by the description of a grand social gathering at a stately palace. Among sophistication and luxury, among nobles and "dignitaries of the church" (9), Howe imagines her entrance as an injection of simplicity and purity. As we see her walking "in serenity of white attire," untouched by the surrounding "tainted atmosphere," and bringing "rosy, the woodland breath of Liberty / From my far home" (10), we are likely to think of Hilda.

Later in the poem, Howe concentrates her attention on monks, who, to her eyes, are the living emblem of the worst evils of the church. Beastly, sensual, idle, and deceitful (17), they are the product of the sins of the past, of a religion turned superstition. It is a characterization we also encounter in *The Marble Faun*, most significantly during the visit to the Church of the Capuchins (chaps. 20–21) and when Donatello considers for a moment the possibility of joining the religious order (chap. 29).

In "Santa Susanna," Howe recalls an experience that bears an interesting resemblance to that of Hilda in chapters 38 and 39 of Hawthorne's romance, when the New England girl takes advantage of the sacrament of the confession. Howe tells in fact of the "silent longing" that led her to enter and seek comfort in a Catholic church, in defiance, one might say, of her Protestant upbringing. She tells of how she immersed her hands in holy water, washed her brow and lips from both material and moral impurities, and then knelt to pray (29). Although Howe's prayer, unlike Hilda's, is addressed, in true Protestant fashion, to God alone, without mediators, she describes this private ritual as her "shrift" (29), as an act of penance that removes the oppressing burden of guilt and uncertainty.

> A sacrifice of expiation sought
> For every wilful error of my life,
> …
> 'Help! raise me from this bed of sloth and shame!'
> Then, silence — then the touch of angels' wings
> Winnowed away that bitter grief and doubt
>
> (29–30)

The image of Rome as a decaying corpse, which Hawthorne uses repeatedly in *The Marble Faun*, may have been suggested by a passage in which Howe describes the city as infested by the spirit of the past, exhaling its cadaverous emanations ("the germ of death / Which" its "decay holds festering in her heart" [19]). But the author's censure of the church in *Passion Flowers* does not necessarily extend to the city of Rome and its people. It is the presence of the spirit of the past, embodied by the church, that suggests the description of the city as a putrefying corpse; but Rome itself, Howe believes, would be "as fragrant as God's Eden" (19) if relieved of that gloomy burden. And there are other things to consider. The hideous presence of monks, for instance, is counterbalanced by the "simplicity" and "integrity" of Jewish rites in the ghetto, where nothing is added or taken away from God's word (18). And although Howe objects to the Jews' wait for the Messiah's coming ("Waiting with infinite loss" [18]), she regards that faith as superior to others in one respect. That faith does preserve "intact" an inestimable lesson, that of the "inviolable unity of God" (19) (in contrast, Hawthorne identifies the ghetto of Rome as the vilest, most corrupted part of the city [1986 (1860), 387–88]).

Examining Howe's attitude toward religion, one notices that the expression of a severe moral judgment does not interfere with her desire for knowledge and contact. Her readers are implicitly exhorted not to trust completely their preestablished views, nor even their direct observation. Catholicism is an aspect of Italian life and, as "Santa Susanna" demonstrates, travelers must be willing to experience even practices that may appear to them objectionable or meaningless. The same is true, in "Rome," of Judaism,[9] which was usually ignored or despised by both Protestants and Catholics.

Similarly, reading Fuller's letters one finds that if, on the one hand, the author is highly critical of Catholicism, on the other she is able to identify with the followers of that creed and to appreciate its ceremonies as cultural manifestations. While never hesitating to condemn the Roman Catholic Church as spiritually impoverished and morally disgraceful, Fuller does, at the same time, register elements of beauty and interest in the scenic apparatus, color, and gestures of its rituals. While referring to the ceremonies as a "gorgeous mummery," she nonetheless confesses that she is "charmed" by their "poetry" and "picture" (243). What is relevant, then, is that her relationship to Catholicism exemplifies her ability to balance opposite impulses (as, in this case, moral objection and emotional association), a skill that expands the scope of her vision. This ability, which colors not only her observations on religion but on other issues as well, accounts for her constant effort to transcend the otherness of Italian culture.

It requires much acquaintance, much thought, much reference to books, for the child of Protestant Republican America to see where belong the legends illustrated by rite and picture, the sense of all the rich tapestry, where it has a united and poetic meaning, where it is broken by some accident of history. For all these things — a senseless mass of juggleries to the uninformed eye — are really growths of the human spirit struggling to develop its life, and full of instruction for those who learn to understand them. (259)

The sensation of having found in Italy a vast field for intellectual and social activity did not blind Fuller to the actual status of her sex in that country. As a serious and thorough correspondent, she could not but inform her readers that an almost generalized lack of instruction kept most Italian women "intellectually in a low place" (262). Nevertheless, if she could not, and would not, alter the facts, she could at least counter-balance them by emphasizing alternative values, illustrious examples from the past, or shining exceptions in the present. Thus, the women's lack of cultural accomplishments was in part redeemed, in Fuller's analysis, by an uncommon display of warmheartedness and courage (as in the chaotic days of the siege of Rome: "women collect the balls from the hostile cannon, and carry them to ours" [406]). These were qualities that through her own experience (as mother, wife of a member of the Republican army, and nurse[10]) she learned to regard as never before in her life. While the reader is invited to reflect on the "depressed" (232) state of woman in Italy, he or she is also reminded that the country's cultural tradition, from antiquity to the recent past, is not devoid of signs of a different reality. It is possible to find them, for instance, in the "noble" representation of female figures in an Etruscan tomb (230), in the legacy of a few women professors at the University of Bologna and at a Milan library, or in the reverence "to the Madonna and innumerable female saints" (232). Fuller was also able to find a living emblem for the future Italian woman to emulate, the perfect figure for the landscape she had conceived: the "revolutionary" Princess Cristina Trivulzio di Belgioioso. Writer, founder of anti-Austrian newspapers, organizer of socialist experiments on her estates, Belgioioso was one of the most active and fascinating protagonists of the Risorgimento[11] and, to Fuller's eyes, the ideal of the fully realized woman (384–85).

As for Howe, it was perhaps as a reaction to the living conditions of Italian women that she imagined Rome as a landscape dominated by female figures. Not only is Rome humanized and gendered (bearer of civilization violated by barbarism [15], or "Queen," "mailed virgin," and "mass-frequenting crone" [36–37]), as one would expect, but also associated with a series of personages — the Sibyl, Iris, Sappho, Juliet — that suggest intensity of sensation.

Even the war, traditionally a theater with men as its sole protagonists, is in Howe's figuration characterized by a prominent female participation. It is up to women, in "From Newport to Rome," to create something positive, a model of solidarity and natural support, out of the havoc of combat:

> 'Those women, gathering on the sward,
> I see them, helpful of each other;
> The matron soothes the maiden's heart,
> The girl supports the trembling mother;
>
> 'Sad recognitions, frantic prayers,
> Greetings that sobs and spasms smother;
> And "Oh my son!" the place resounds,
> And "Oh my father! oh my brother!"
>
> (64–65)

It is to women, significantly viewed as the natural repositories of the values of brotherhood and empathy, that the poem's most urgent appeal is directed:

> 'With fuller light, let women's eyes,
> Earnest, beneath the Christ-like brow,
> Strike this deep question home to men,
> "Thy brothers perish — idlest thou?"
>
> 'With warmer breath, let mothers' lips
> Whisper the boy whom they caress, —
> "Learn from those arms that circle thee
> In love, to succor, shelter, bless."
>
> (66–67)

The value of courage — which, as we have seen, both Fuller and Howe claim as a feminine virtue — is not only illustrated in their works but also, and more significantly, by them. The construction of Italy as a territory, as a frontier, constitutes itself a form of courage. It implies, on the part of the authors, a willingness to take chances, to abandon the caution of the mere traveler for the curiosity and open-mindedness of the explorer.

# 2

## Confronting the Mystery:
## Nathaniel Hawthorne's *The Marble Faun* (1860)

While obviously related to observations and experiences occasioned by his January 1858–May 1859 Italian sojourn, Hawthorne's use of setting in *The Marble Faun* (1860) is also a development of themes and questions first addressed in his 1846 tale "Rappaccini's Daughter." On a first impression, there would seem to be a not insignificant difference in point of view between the two works: in the earlier work, Giovanni Guasconti, the protagonist and principal observer, is presented as an Italian interacting with his fellow countrymen in an Italian city. Yet, as we are informed at the beginning of the story, he is a southerner who has come to study in the northern city of Padua. If we consider the great cultural differences between the two parts of Italy at the time of the story (usually identified as the first half of the sixteenth century), we may consider Giovanni almost as much a foreigner as are Kenyon and Hilda of *The Marble Faun*. Like them, he is "out of his native sphere" (1974 [1846], 93) and confronted with new, unfamiliar surroundings and manners that test both his emotional balance and perception of reality.

Giovanni's primary object of observation is a beautiful young woman, Beatrice Rappaccini. The intimations of mystery and danger associated with her reappear, I believe, in *The Marble Faun* in the characterization of Miriam (who, as we discover at the end of the romance, is half Italian) and the depiction of Rome and Italy. Giovanni's impressions of Beatrice, whether well founded or imaginary, center on the dualism of beauty and death as embodied by the gorgeous but poisonous shrub with which she is repeatedly identified. Similarly, in *The Marble Faun*, a sense of impending peril is early associated with the charm and loveliness of Miriam and the city of Rome. Trying to warn Donatello of the possible harm to which he exposes himself by following her, Miriam seems to describe sinister consequences that may result from simple physical contact or proximity with her person: "Those who come too near me are in danger of great mischiefs, I do assure you. Take warning, therefore!" (81).[1] She tries to make him see that she is indeed no less dangerous than the Roman air they breathe in the beautiful grounds of the Villa Borghese, that air that is as gentle and languid as it is insidious because "full of malaria" (80). Nor is language the only medium through which Miriam characterizes herself as potentially harmful to others. As a painter, she chooses as subjects such violent and disquieting figures as Judith, Jael, and Salome, thus making the theme of female threat to men central to her art.

The source of the evil Miriam sees as constantly accompanying her is to be found in her personal history, just as the "influence" that makes the Roman air "deadly to human lungs" (90) originates in the city's dark and bloody past. Furthermore, the past is inescapable: that of Miriam, personified by a sinister-looking character (the man she used as her model when painting), literally follows her at every step. That of the city meets the visitor's eye in every direction, with its innumerable traces: ruins, buildings, paintings, sculptures, etc. It is an unbearably daunting presence and yet not devoid, as it appears, of a strange, repellent charm. For what is the visit to the catacomb of St. Calixtus (chap. 3) if not a quest for the past? It is during that underground descent by torchlight, through narrow passages and along niches still covered with ashes and bones, that Miriam encounters the man who, from that moment, becomes her persecutor.

> "Henceforth, I am nothing but a shadow behind her footsteps. She came to me when I sought her not. She has called me forth, and must abide the conse-quences of my re-appearance in the world." (31)

Miriam's passive demeanor toward the mysterious individual seems to suggest that the lure the past exercises upon us may lead to a terrible form of thraldom. It is a condition that suffocates life and can only be relieved through a radical act of liberation. For Miriam, this act finds ultimate expression in the unconscious sign of assent with which her eyes sanction and direct Donatello's murder (or, one might say, execution) of her model. Rome — indeed, the whole country — we are repeatedly reminded, would probably profit from an equally violent destruction of the past. As things are, the past weighs heavily on the present, with its formidable mass of wrongs and sins.

As we accompany Kenyon and Donatello through a street of an ancient Tuscan town (chap. 32), the narrator remarks that "nothing can exceed the grim ugliness of the houses ... gray, dilapidated, or half-covered with plaster in patches" (293). What makes the aspect of these buildings particularly disquieting is their solidity, their "appearance of ponderous durability" (301), which seems to condemn them to a perpetual decay. Nature, the narrator also observes, is "as much shut out from the one street of the rustic village as from the heart of any swarming city" (293). This absence inevitably renders the sense of the past more oppressive, as nothing that meets the eye suggests the idea of renewal or rebirth.

The rude stone buildings of rural Tuscany are contrasted with the neat wooden houses of New England. Of all the signs in the landscape, the house is perhaps the most pregnant, and Hawthorne uses it effectively to propose an aesthetic and moral evaluation of two societies. The "dark and half-ruinous habitations" (293) of the Italian countryside tell of a vicious and hopeless world that is in direct opposition to the sound values and prosperity that the narrator associates with the cheerful appearance of his own country's dwellings. The structure and conformation of the Italian buildings is considered primarily in terms of sensations, of their emotional impact on the observer. They are presented as generically representative expressions of the local use of space and the local idea of family and community. What is bypassed, however, is their specificity as peasant households and the all-important correlation between their external aspect and their function. As Turri has pointed out, the Italian rural dwelling is to be viewed as shaped to the exigencies, practices, and rhythms of agricultural work and revealing plainly the activity of those who inhabit it (1983, 220). For Hawthorne,

> neither the wretched cottages nor the dreary farm-houses seemed to partake of the prosperity, with which so kindly a climate, and so fertile a portion of Mother Earth's bosom, should have filled them, one and all.... The Italians appear to possess none of that emulative pride which we see in our New England villages, where every householder, according to his taste and means, endeavours to make his homestead an ornament to the grassy and elm-

shadowed wayside. In Italy, there are no neat door-steps and thresholds; no pleasant, vine-sheltered porches; none of those grass-plots or smoothly shorn lawns, which hospitably invite the imagination into the sweet domestic interiors of English life. (295–96)

Compared with New England dwellings, Tuscan cottages and farm-houses appear to the narrator ugly, miserable, and uninviting. They cannot possibly satisfy his requirements, which are essentially those of an urban and bourgeois culture. They cannot fit into a system of values where the house is chiefly intended as an exhibition of one's social status (Turri 1983, 220).

The author's tender, affectionate tone in evoking his native landscape is more than an expression of simple homesickness. One detects also a sense of apprehension, perhaps an awareness that what is described is imperiled. More than one critic (such as Matthiessen and, recently, Levine and Schumaker) has already considered the "pre-Civil War" climate characterizing the publication of *The Marble Faun* in 1860. The text has been said to contain intimations of the traumatic changes that were to affect American life as a result of that event (in Conrad Schumaker's words, "we never really see Hilda and Kenyon in America because the country for which they departed would never exist" [1984, 83]). Accordingly, the passage I have just cited may be seen as a last farewell to a world of homely urbanity and gentleness that was soon to be wiped away by the tensions and energies of the great conflict. In the years following the war, a much harsher economic competitiveness would replace the one expressed through the domestic pride of Hawthorne's New England villagers.

As Nathalia Wright has justly observed, Kenyon is "thinking of America" (1965, 160) when, during a conversation with Donatello's old butler at Monte Beni, he identifies the world's growing sadness as the result of an increasingly utilitarian approach to life.

It is the iron rule in our days, to require an object and a purpose in life. It makes us all parts of a complicated scheme of progress, which can only result in our arrival at a colder and drearier region than we were born in. It insists upon everybody's adding somewhat (a mite, perhaps, but earned by incessant effort) to an accumulated pile of usefulness, of which the only use will be, to burthen our posterity with even heavier thoughts and more inordinate labor than our own. (Hawthorne 1986 [1860], 239)

A little earlier in the romance, Kenyon is given a chance to savor —
quite literally — the product of a view of life completely antithetical to
the one just described. The ambrosia-like wine that Donatello offers his
American friend is not made to be sold but to be shared with the household's guests. Quoting an old family tradition, the butler tells Kenyon
that, were the Sunshine wine of Monte Beni (as that precious nectar is
called) to be sent to the market, it would "lose all its wonderful qualities"
(224). Though perhaps sadder and wiser than of old, Donatello's world is
still capable of bringing forth a creation of pure enjoyment such as this
one. On the contrary, to judge from Kenyon's somber reflections, no
such sunshine was in sight that could filter through the gloomy clouds
crowding the American scene.

The episode just mentioned stands out in a book in which drink and
food are for the most part described as sharing in the nastiness the author
often attributes to the Italian population. The wine Kenyon drinks while
on his way to Perugia is apparently a far cry from that of Monte Beni,
since it has to be abundantly "diluted with water from the fountain" to
become tolerable (294). But it is in Rome, not surprisingly, that all sorts
of provisions appear to have been contaminated by the wickedness of the
place (consider, for instance, the "sour bread, sour wine, rancid butter,
and bad cookery, needlessly bestowed on evil meats," of chapter 36,
p. 326, or the "wine of dolorous acerbity" of chapter 46, p. 418). Just like
the continuous references to filth, such comments on food and drink aim
at making the evil of the city visible, concrete, and physically
apprehensible.

A crucial effect of the imposing presence of the past in Italy is that it
gives the present an "evanescent and visionary" (6) quality. This singular
character of the Italian atmosphere is seen in the romance as one of the
strongest sources of attraction for the numerous foreign artists residing in
the country. The suggestion, it would appear, is that they view their
endeavors as belonging most appropriately in a sort of ideal realm. It is
as inhabitants of that sphere that they become "free citizens" (132).

What needs also to be considered, as the narrator reminds us, is their
sheer number. In Italy, in Rome in particular, the artists find themselves
"in force." They are not in the condition of "isolated strangers," as in the
"unsympathizing cities of their native land." Although the artists
Hawthorne refers to here are primarily painters and sculptors (looking
back in dismay at "their lonely studios" [132]), it is perhaps not pushing

a point too far to assume that his considerations apply to writers as well. In addition, one is strongly tempted to replace the general term "foreigners" with that of "Americans." One can then read this part of the book as suggesting indirectly that the artist is, in a way, almost out of place in a country like America, where "actualities are so strongly insisted upon" (3). There, perhaps, the water power of the Fountain of Trevi would be employed "to turn the machinery of a cotton mill" (146).

It is the artist in Hawthorne who is most forcefully attracted by Rome. It is his sense of belonging there that counterbalances the perception of evil and decay. After a blasting tirade against the corpse-like city, her "crooked, intricate streets," "yellow-washed hovels," and "pretence of holiness and reality of nastiness," as well as the "desolation of her ruin, and the hopelessness of her future" (325–26), the narrator goes on to explain that

> when we have left Rome in such mood as this, we are astonished by the discovery, by-and-by, that our heart-strings have mysteriously attached themselves to the Eternal City, and are drawing us thitherward again, as if it were more familiar, more intimately our home, than even the spot where we were born! (326)

But is this Rome a real place? Not if we conceive of a city as made of people as much as of buildings and atmospheres. Romans are as good as banned from Hawthorne's "Eternal City." For him, as for many other foreign artists, the inhabitants of the city, with their "real," obtrusive movements, voices, and noises, spoil the scene. They, not the foreign visitors, are the real intruders. They constitute such an annoying, incongruous presence in reality that excluding them from one's fantasy becomes a sort of satisfying compensation. It is hardly surprising, as Guido Fink has observed, that there are "very few Italian living characters in the American novels set in Rome." Donatello, in his view, "is no exception, being a statue that comes to life like a golem" (1990, 303).

Of the four principal characters in *The Marble Faun*, Donatello is the only one who is not an artist. Rather, he is often observed, even scrutinized, by his three friends as if he were an art object. While his relationships with Miriam and Kenyon have been widely explored, very little attention has been devoted to the relationship between him and Hilda. The reason, simply stated, is that there is no interaction whatsoever between the two. They never talk to each other[2] and never meet without their two friends. Hilda does discuss and comment *on* Donatello with both Miriam and Kenyon, but she never addresses him directly (though it is clear, from the story, that she has mastered at least some Italian). As for Donatello, most of the time he seems hardly aware of Hilda's existence. From the beginning there is a barrier between them that is not related to the sin-and-guilt theme of the story. They are kept separate because they are the ultimate representatives of their respective cultures, of worlds the author indicates as irreconcilable.

It is well to notice how Hawthorne, while often assaulting Rome (both as place and human community), does at the same time subtly undermine the reliability of such outbursts by having them coincide in the narration with moments of great crisis and emotional instability for his two American characters. It is through the eyes of Hilda, oppressed by the knowledge of the terrible secret of Miriam and Donatello, that we see the art masterpieces of the city's galleries become diminished. They no longer seem the immortal works she had once thought them to be. It is because of the new sensitivity and perception with which grief and hopelessness endow her that she becomes acutely aware of the general "deficiency of earnestness and absolute truth" in Italian pictures "after the art had become consummate" (338). It is a loss of reverence for art that makes her penetrate "the canvas like a steel probe" and find "but a crust of paint over an emptiness" (341).

The narrator, in part interpreting, in part bringing to extremes the implications of Hilda's state of mind, puts into question the achievements and the very significance of centuries of Italian painting. We are confronted with the suggestion that, perhaps, the "mighty Italian masters" were profoundly lacking in humanity, since their work appealed not to "human sympathies, but to a false intellectual taste, which they themselves were the first to create" (336). In addition, we are reminded of the repetitiousness of their subjects, both religious and mythological, and the impropriety of their eclecticism: their brush passing without difficulty from the depiction of a Madonna with child, or a crucifixion, to that of a nude Venus or Leda. With no other merit than those of mere aesthetic character, their works are reduced to the status of mere artifacts and, as such, are better destined to oblivion:

> One picture in ten thousand, perhaps, ought to live in the applause of mankind, from generation to generation, until the colours fade and blacken

out of sight, or the canvas rot entirely away. For the rest, let them be piled in garrets, just as the tolerable poets are shelved, when their little day is over. Is a painter more sacred than a poet? (341)

Later in the romance, we follow Kenyon as he wanders dejectedly through the city in search of Hilda, who has apparently vanished into thin air. It is through the "darkly coloured medium of his fears" (411) that Rome becomes a sort of netherworld, the quintessential abode of evil, with "no redeeming element, such as exists in other dissolute and wicked cities" (411). The evil Kenyon sees around him has been fortified and intensified through centuries of crime and guilt, permeating every single stone, "rising foglike from the ancient depravity of Rome, and brooding over the dead and half-rotten city, as nowhere on earth" (412). Not surprisingly, the population of such a city is described as having "no genuine belief in virtue" (411) and being always ready (thanks to the clever ritual of the confession) to pass from one sin to the next as unburdened by remorse as ever.

This part of the romance includes an interesting reference to the presence of a foreign occupying force in the city. The French soldiers are described as the new barbarians (an expression, as I indicated in the Introduction, that is currently used in Italy to refer to all foreign tourists), the "inheritors of the foul license" (412) exercised in previous ages by Gauls, Goths, and Vandals. Yet there is no clear indication that the Romans suffer directly from this oppression, and this condemnation of the conquerors does not bring forth a sentiment of sympathy for the plight of the conquered. On the contrary, the almost inescapable impression is that the "foul license" of the French, far from making them appear as lawless usurpers, perfectly matches the surrounding corruption. Unlike Margaret Fuller and Julia Ward Howe, Hawthorne does not perceive the presence of the French army in terms of invasion, violation, or betrayal, but rather as a natural manifestation of the moral malady of the city. It is a malady that invests all strata of society, from the nobility down to the lower classes and, of course, the church.

The narrator's observations on the French army here represent one of the rare instances in which the political situation of Rome is referred to. Indeed, I would go so far as to argue that the reader of *The Marble Faun* may even fail to realize that the city described in the romance is under occupation. It seems to me that, rather than "continually" reminding us of the "coercive presence throughout Rome of the French military" (as Robert S. Levine has maintained [1990, 25]), Hawthorne more often than not downplays it or treats it as an unimportant part of the background. It is a significant choice on his part, especially considering that in his journal, which contains the germs of many episodes of the story, he not only observes that the French soldiers "are prominent objects everywhere about the city," but also that "they serve as an efficient police, making Rome as safe as London [Hawthorne's idea of a civilized city], whereas, without them, it would very likely be a den of banditti" (63–64).

The Rome of *The Marble Faun* is a city that might have never seen the revolution of 1849 or lived the hectic months of the republic. What we find of the political milieu of the period is only the atmosphere of oppression and surveillance created by the papal government. Moreover, if, as Levine (1990) and Goldman (1984) (among others) have observed, it is true that Hawthorne repeatedly emphasizes and denounces the pervasive influence of the church over the life of the city I believe that such a critique is not grounded in the specificity of the historical period in which the story is set. Given that the city Hawthorne depicts is strictly ruled by an absolutist government, it is clear that he never conceives of its inhabitants as those upon whom such a yoke is imposed. Rather than being presented as the victims of despotism, they appear to find in their state of subjection and mutual mistrust their natural condition.

As observed by Kenyon during his frantic search for Hilda (chap. 45), the wanton and dissolute French soldiers that patrol Rome are part of the darkness that may have engulfed his pure and innocent loved one. But a far more threatening and repugnant image is that of a "priesthood pampered, sensual, with red and bloated cheeks, and carnal eyes" (411).[3] Kenyon's view, the narrator warns us, is "morbid" (412), colored by fear and anger. It represents only one facet of Hawthorne's own view, which is complex and, at times, ambivalent. Hawthorne does on a few occasions refer to the pure spirituality that characterized the origins of Catholicism. On the other hand, there are many times in which he implies that, because of what he sees as the church's strong ties with paganism, Catholicism has always been a travesty of religion. To make matters even more intricate, there is also the question of what Hawthorne describes as the "infinite convenience" of this faith to "its devout believers" (355). What he indicates by such an expression is the way in which the church, in its long history, has constantly adapted its rituals and rules to accommodate the needs and difficulties of its followers. There are moments in which Hawthorne appears to suggest that, perhaps, Catholicism has an edge over Protestantism in that it understands human weakness and forgives it. Yet, often in the romance, one encounters a strongly contrasting view, according to which such understanding and adaptability are but a shameless surrender of ethics, as opposed to the wholesome severity of the Reformed Churches. At times, this ambivalence finds expression in a narrative tone in which irony coexists with admiration.

Commenting on the "miraculous" functionality of Catholicism, the narrator observes that "it is difficult to imagine it a contrivance of mere man" (345). Uncertain whether to define it as divine or diabolic, Hawthorne is at once fascinated and disgusted by a religion that applies "itself to all human occasions" (346). It is a tension that reaches its climax with Hilda's spiritual crisis, as we follow her in her painful pilgrimage from church to church and finally see her kneel in a confessional at St. Peter's. Devoured by the secret she carries within her, the young woman cannot but notice the number of ways in which Catholics can find relief from their inner torments.

In a church, a young man gives vent to his grief after a confession of guilt to his patron, and the narrator observes that if the "youth had been a Protestant, he would have kept all that torture pent up in his heart, and let it burn there till it seared him into indifference" (347). The shrines and chapels of the Virgin that meet Hilda's eyes, almost at every step, make her wonder whether her own faith should have "a woman to listen to the prayers of women" (348). As we reach St. Peter's, Hawthorne's emphasis shifts to the seductive power of space, color, and light, suggesting once again that spirituality in Italy is inseparable from aesthetic response.

> The pavement! ... [T]he roof! the Dome! Rich, gorgeous, filled with sunshine.... [T]hose lofty depths seemed to translate the heavens to mortal comprehension, and help the spirit upward to a yet higher and wider sphere. Must not the Faith, that built this matchless edifice, and warmed, illuminated, and overflowed from it, include whatever can satisfy human aspirations, at the loftiest, or minister to human necessity at the sorest! If religion had a material home, was it not here! (351)

It is in a state of rapture and bewilderment, brought about by the immensity and chromatic brilliance of the cathedral, that Hilda approaches a confessional and, to use Hawthorne's expression, "avails"

(359) herself of the sacrament of penance. Although the young woman experiences what is described as a form of rebirth, the episode must not be interpreted as implicitly dismissing former reservations about the Catholic faith. Hawthorne's dilemma remains unresolved, as he is ultimately unable to choose between that religion and Protestantism. Hilda is saved by her confession. Significantly, however, she refuses to recognize it as a religious act. She considers providential the impulse that brought her to St. Peter's, but she loses no time, after she emerges from the confessional, to reaffirm her loyalty to her Protestant upbringing ("I am a daughter of the Puritans" [362]). Yet, questioned by Kenyon a few moments later, she expresses a great sense of uncertainty. Her tentative willingness to recognize the advantages of Catholicism now contrasts deeply with the severity of the sculptor and, perhaps, it is in the unlikely combination of their views that Hawthorne's own perplexity finds expression.

> *Hilda.* Really, I do not quite know what I am.... Why should not I be a Catholic, if I find there what I need, and what I cannot find elsewhere? The more I see of this worship, the more I wonder at the exuberance with which it adapts itself to all the demands of human infirmity....
>
> *Kenyon.* The exceeding ingenuity of the system stamps it as the contrivance of man, or some worse author, not an emanation of the broad and simple wisdom from on high." (368)

It is a desire to preserve the best of two contrasting attitudes that seems to be manifested through the transformation of Hilda's character in the final part of the romance: in the way in which, while acquiring the warmth and softness that make her learn, at least, to accept Kenyon's love, she retains nonetheless an adamant sternness of judgment as regards the separation of rights and wrongs.

If Margaret Fuller's letters and Julia Ward Howe's poems suggest a view of their authors' Italian sojourns as a form of exploration and conquest, *The Marble Faun* appears to present travel as a metaphorical loss of ground. Except for Miriam, who, I insist, is strongly identified with the city of Rome, the major characters of the book are all displaced. For Kenyon and Hilda, nothing could be more different from their native New England than Rome, but fairly great is also the distance (and not only the one we can measure) separating that city and Donatello's birthplace in Tuscany. Although apparently consisting of a series of new experiences and discoveries, their Roman life does not seem to be characterized by acquisitions or gains but rather by threats to their mental and emotional stability, if not to their very identity (and Hilda's uncertainties about religion may be interpreted in this sense). In Tuscany, Donatello was a beloved young nobleman; in Rome, he becomes first an art object, then a murderer, and finally a penitent. As for the two young Americans, their greatest fear appears to be that of being "possessed" by the city, absorbed by it. As a form of protection, they seek to create a distance between themselves and the place (living in a tower or among the whiteness of marble).

It is perhaps because of this same fear that Hawthorne ultimately holds back and does not attempt to illuminate the otherness of Rome or, more generally, of Italy. Italy remains invariably mysterious and, like Kenyon during the carnival, Hawthorne is unable to participate in the spectacle he narrates. On the other hand, *The Marble Faun* makes it clear that being a part of the scene, ceasing to be a spectator to become an actor/anthropologist, would be dangerous. The American who, after living intensely the Italian experience, decides to return home, may discover that she or he has undergone a sad transformation (*Transformation*, as is well known, is the English title of *The Marble Faun*): far from becoming more American, as Margaret Fuller ardently believed, the traveler may have become a foreigner in both places, having only, in Hawthorne's words, "that little space of either, in which we finally lay down our discontented bones" (461).

# 3

## Different Views of a City:
## James Fenimore Cooper's *The Bravo* (1831)
## and William Dean Howells's
## *Venetian Life* (1866)

The mask motif figures prominently in James Fenimore Cooper's *The Bravo* (1831) and William Dean Howells's *Venetian Life* (1866), but with different implications in each case. Cooper's novel, set in Venice in the early eighteenth century, evokes a period in which the city's inhabitants wore masks for about six months a year. In the theaters, a masked audience watched performers whose features were likewise disguised. As in a room of mirrors, mystery reflected mystery. But the most formidable mask, Cooper maintains in *The Bravo*, was not made of pasteboard, like the theatrical "Bautta."[1] Rather, it consisted of a simple word, the denomination "republic," by which the government of Venice defined itself, for the real face of the establishment was that of an absolutist oligarchy.

Howells's work is also about unmasking, about bringing to light the real nature of things. The camouflage that, in the author's intentions, needed to be removed from the city of Venice was the one imposed by a particular literary tradition. Describing with exactness the look and sound of Venetian life, Howells tried to do justice to the everyday aspect of the city and to refute "false beliefs that had become commonplaces" (Battilana 1989, 106). His was a reaction against the fallacies and myths popularized by such authors as Byron and Rogers. What he proposed was a method of representation based on authenticity and accuracy.

59

What we find portrayed in Cooper's *The Bravo* is neither a verisimilar eighteenth-century Venice nor, in a sense, the city he saw in 1830 during a brief visit (ten days). The Venice Cooper experienced then could not accord completely with the kind of atmosphere he intended to create. It could not quite represent what Cooper associated with the Venetian republic: a place dominated by a dreaded, omnipresent force, constantly keeping surveillance over the acts and thoughts of its citizens. What he could use of the actual impact of the city on him was that odd mixture of wonder and disquiet that often characterizes the response of first-time visitors. As Sergio Bettini has remarked, the stranger in Venice "cannot but feel unbalanced, removed from the quiet dimensions of his normal state in the world.... He experiences rapture, but also a secret uneasiness" (Battilana 1989, 99).

Unlike Rome and Florence, Venice in the first half of the nineteenth century was not a place where American travelers usually resided for months or years. They just passed through it, and the city generally remained, to their eyes, eminently strange, almost unearthly. This, in Cooper's case, was an advantage. It gave him freedom to reinvent the city, to create a proper setting for his novel on the basis of vague sensations and literary reminiscences rather than on fidelity to detail.

Howells, on the contrary, made the most of his condition of resident (for three and a half years) to annotate painstakingly the city's ordinary experience. Developing what we might call an anthropological aesthetic, he conceived *Venetian Life* as a study of a people's mores and their environment rather than as a simple travel guide. It was his conviction that Venetian reality, as it was, offered enough interest, charm, and even mystery. To add anything more would mean to disfigure it. One can see how, with few adjustments, the same principle might be extended to any society and its portrayal, even in fiction.

### The Bravo

In the course of his long Italian sojourn (nine months in Florence, five in Naples and Sorrento, and five in Rome, all from October 1828 to May 1830), Cooper devoted but a brief span of time to the exploration of Venice. Yet, as he recalls in his *Gleanings in Europe: Italy* (1837), that city had a strong impact on his sensibility. He was fascinated by its environmental and topographical singularity and by its character of meeting point of Western and Eastern cultures. Recollecting his first walk through the city, he wrote: "No other place ever struck my imagination so forcibly; and never before did I experience so much pleasure, from novel objects, in so short a time" (1981, 280–81). Indeed, the description of the city in *Gleanings* insistently qualifies the observer's experience as something unparalleled, unexpected, and almost inexpressible. Nothing Cooper had seen during his Italian sojourn had quite prepared him for the distinctive aspect and atmosphere of Venice. What the "Venetian" pages of *Gleanings* admirably convey is precisely Cooper's initial surprise and fascination, but it is in *The Bravo*[2] that one finds the outcome, the "evidence," as it were, of that first impression.

The term "imagination" is central to Cooper's use of setting in the novel.[3] Throughout *The Bravo*, the scene of the action is suggested rather than illuminated, it is sketched rather than drawn. Joy S. Kasson has justly observed that *The Bravo*, unlike *The Marble Faun*, "could not be used as a guidebook by tourists in search of monuments" (1982, 152). The aspect of Venice in Cooper's novel is altered, reimagined, and scarcely recognizable. Representing a city he had known only superficially, the author did not reproduce landscapes and buildings. Instead, he concentrated on rendering what, for him, was the feeling of the place. If then, on the one hand, it is often difficult to follow and visualize the characters' movements, on the other, one is made constantly aware of the state of political and moral decadence of the city. Cooper cannot make us see the Ducal Palace and the other places of power, but he communicates distinctly a sense of tired greatness, of oppressive immobility, that is perfectly suited to a former empire in rapid decline. Through his recurrent use of such qualifiers as "heavy," "massive," and "grand," both the city as a whole and its various palaces take on the appearance of awe-inspiring but moribund pachyderms.

Despite its diminished international standing, the Venetian state portrayed in *The Bravo* is still quite a formidable political machine. Its control over the lives of its subjects is so complete, its methods so insidious, that it suggests a pervasive malignant force (rather significantly, both Marius Bewley [1959, 58] and Donald A. Ringe [1963, 12–13] have drawn parallels between *The Bravo* and George Orwell's *1984*). Beside the mask, to which I referred earlier, other recurring thematic elements indicate the inscrutable character of Venice's powerful institutions.

Describing a patrician dwelling, Cooper calls our attention to its many entrances and maze-like interior, the deceptive play of light and shadow,[4] the curtains, the mirrors, and, in particular, the mosaic floors (with their composite form of "curiously embedded" marbles from East and West [58]).[5] Every object, every architectural detail, tells of the distance between appearance and reality. Externally, the palace shows its "different faces," including the one reflected by the canal over which it looks out. As the narrator notes, the building "literally" rises "from out the water" (58), confronting its visitors with its enigmatic aspect (the same, of course, also applies to the whole city, with the lagoon functioning very much like a gigantic looking glass). Its real nature, like that of the power it represents, is very difficult to penetrate. Elaborating on Adrian Stokes's observations on the mysterious quality of Venetian buildings, William M. Johnston has rightly noted how, especially on the Grand Canal, the particular aspect of Venetian façades invites "prying glances from gondolas below" (1987, 73).

At times, in *The Bravo*, the suggestion is that the entire urban structure of Venice, with its intricate pattern of narrow streets and waterways, visualizes the web of intrigue and wickedness of the state. Such an ideological use of the landscape, of the particular modification and utilization of nature of which Venice is the result, has to be regarded as strictly related to the political purpose of the novel. It is in line with the author's presentation of eighteenth-century Venice as a negative example, a warning (what a republic may degenerate into) for nineteenth-century America. It constitutes, in my view, a highly effective but potentially ambiguous strategy. The topographical conformation of a city is undoubtedly a powerful visual equivalent of a government's political conduct. Yet, because it represents quite a broad canvas, its import may easily exceed the limits intended by the author. In other words, what is supposedly attributed to a certain political system in a certain historical period may be seen as extending, in general, to a people's character. *The Bravo* may give the impression, that is, of demonizing Venice, of questioning its entire historical and cultural significance.

I believe the possible identification of such a subtext to be a factor that deserves to be taken into account when we look at certain hostile reactions to Cooper's novel on the part of contemporary Italian reviewers. Let us consider, for example, the article that Venetian novelist and critic Pietro Zorzi wrote for the *Indicatore Lombardo* in January of 1835. In it,

Zorzi, a former admirer of Cooper's work, bitterly complained that it was impossible to enumerate all the "absurdities and errors" (1) contained in the novel (a view echoed, that same year, by Gaetano Barbieri in the *Raccoglitore italiano e straniero*). He contested, among other things, the historical accuracy of central elements in the plot, such as the presence of bravos in Venice, the range of powers of the Venetian Senate, and the practice, on the part of that institution, of assuming the guardianship of wealthy noble heiresses (such as the heroine of the tale, Donna Violetta) for political purposes. On the basis of questionable sources (such as Daru's *Histoire de la République de Venise*, 1829) and the "gossips of the ciceroni"·of the Ducal Palace, *The Bravo* reinforced the dark legend surrounding Venetian rulers. Equally unpardonable was the way in which Cooper had blundered in portraying "customs, uses, and places." Zorzi could only comment ironically on certain topographical inventions and refused to recognize his "lively" fellow citizens in the "ghosts" (1) that inhabited Cooper's Venice. As concerns, specifically, Cooper's characterizations, it is fair to assume that it was not only the portrayal of Venetians as joyless and suspicious people that irritated Zorzi. Although he did not state it openly, I suspect he also reacted against the presence — and use — in the text of a series of overexploited topoi. What Rosella Mamoli Zorzi has described as Cooper's preference for the Venice "of the Gothic and literary tradition" over the city "he had actually seen" (1990, 297) emerges not only in his representation of place but of people as well.

Since the opening description of St. Mark's Square, the observing eye is revealed to be that of a stranger at the theater[6] ("the hurried air and careless eye; the measured step and jealous glance; the jest and laugh; ... the grimace of the buffoon, and the tragic frown of the improvisatore" [Cooper 1963, 19]). The impression is repeatedly confirmed throughout the novel by the terms with which the Italian character is described: "impetuosity" (157), "warm fancies, fervent minds" (167), "energy of language and feeling" (230), "fervor" (244), "force of expression" (361), etc. The words chosen by Cooper evoke physical rather than psychological traits: there is no correspondence between them and the characters to which they are referred. We are told that a certain figure possesses "Italian impetuosity and fervor," but this is not what his or her characterization expresses. As a consequence, words supposedly indicating typical Italian qualities remain little more than labels that only emphasize the distance between the author and his subject matter.

About a century after the publication of Pietro Zorzi's review, one finds the same mixture of indignation and irony in Angelina La Piana's *La cultura americana e l'Italia* (1938). In the chapter on Cooper, La Piana brings to the surface an idea that was possibly latent in the article by her predecessor. She argues, in fact, that both characters and setting in *The Bravo* are only superficially Venetian and in reality American. In her view, Jacopo Frontoni, the title's "bravo" (a "hired assassin"), recalls closely the Indians of Cooper's frontier novels. Indeed, he is a sort of "immigrant" who has left the shores of the Great Lakes for the city of Venice. Able-bodied, somber, taciturn, and shrewd, he moves furtively through the narrow streets of the city as if they were his native forests and prairies; or glides through the canals in a gondola which he maneuvers just as deftly as he would a canoe (257, 256). More recently, adopting a similar approach, Alberta Fabris Grube has described the character of the old fisherman Antonio as being "too American" by reason of his natural confidence in the possibility of asserting his rights (1969, 44).

I believe the pleasure of recognition to be largely, but not totally, denied to the modern Italian reader of *The Bravo*. It is not impossible to find isolated instances in which Cooper's characters and situations sound interestingly familiar. Such is the case with the dialogue between the Calabrian mariner Stefano Milano and the Venetian gondolier Gino Monaldi[7] in chapter 1. Monaldi's irritated retort to his friend's observations on the rapidly decreasing power of Venice well illustrates the habit of looking back in time to refute a disagreeable reality. As I have pointed out in the Introduction, a stubborn expression of pride in a country's past (or, as in this case, a city's) is not inhibited but rather galvanized by the inescapable evidence of decay in the present.[8]

> "Thou hast been much, of late, among the lying Genoese, Stefano, that thou comest hither with these idle tales of what a heretic can do. Genova la Superba! What has a city of walls to compare with one of canals and islands like this? — and what has that Apennine republic performed, to be put in comparison with the great deeds of the Queen of the Adriatic? Thou forgettest that Venezia has been —

> "Zitto, zitto! that *has* been, caro mio, is a great word with all Italy. Thou art as proud of the past as a Roman of the Trastevere." (29)

Monaldi's words show how identity, to use Bollati's phrase, "is defined by difference" (1989, 955). The uniqueness of Venice is defended through a comparison with its traditional rival, Genoa, whose very structure ("a city of walls") qualifies it as the perfect antithesis of the "Serenissima." Less "authentic" appears instead the point of view expressed through the character of Milano. The impression of foreignness conveyed by his answer (his referring to a "favorite Italian expression" as if he did not identify with that culture) is confirmed in the following paragraph. In reply to the Venetian's proud evocation of past glories and gestures, he declares that it is better to be "one of a people which is great and victorious just now" (29). Clearly, the allusion is not to Milano's own Calabria (that certainly could not advance such a claim at that time), but rather to Cooper's countrymen.

Nor is this the only instance in which the present, the time of the author and his audience, makes an incursion into the narration. The effect of such "invasions" is that of reinforcing the connotation of the story as exemplum, of identifying similarities and contrasts between distant experiences (the world of the characters versus the world of the readers). The author reiterates two crucial messages in the course of the narrative. On the one hand, he insists on the effort that the members of a democratic society (such as the United States) must make in order to comprehend the distorted, degraded institutions described in the novel. It is a way to show how fortunate and advantageous is, potentially, the state of things in America, how wise the nation's sociopolitical order.

> It may be well to explain, here, to the reader, some of the peculiar machinery of the state, in the country of which we write ... for the name of a republic ... may have induced him to believe that there was, at least, a resemblance between the outlines of that government, and the more just, because more popular, institutions of his own country. (144–45)

> Less odium was attached to men of that class [assassins], in Italy and at that day, than will be easily imagined in a country like this; for the radical defects and the vicious administration of the laws, caused an irritable and sensitive people too often to take into their own hands, the right of redressing their own wrongs. (228)

On the other hand, he intimates that even such a privileged condition is not immune from peril. Through his representation of a state that was a republic in name only, Cooper intended to warn his countrymen of the consequences they would face if they abandoned their original democratic principles in favor of iniquitous foreign models. As Donald A. Ringe has pointed out, *The Bravo* is an attack on "the aristocracy of England, who Cooper believed ruled the country in their own selfish interests, and the Doctrinaires of France, who wanted to establish a similarly aristocratic system under Louis Philippe's monarchy" (1990, 6).

The lesson to be drawn from the state of things in eighteenth-century Venice, as illustrated by Cooper, is that when make-believe prevails over truth, and materialism ("this money-getting age" [91]) triumphs over principle, even a powerful and apparently solid establishment can collapse or be utterly transformed.

> At the period of which we write, that ambitious, crapulous, and factitious state was rather beginning to feel the symptomatic evidence of its fading circumstances, than to be fully conscious of the swift progress of a downward course. In this manner do communities, like individuals, draw near their dissolution, inattentive to the symptoms of decay, until they are overtaken with that fate which finally overwhelms empires and their power in the common lot of man. (107)

Through the character of the old fisherman Antonio and his contacts with Venetian authority, Cooper explores the relationship between the powerless and the powerful. Antonio's unsuccessful appeals to the highest representatives of the state (Senator Grandenigo, the doge, the Council of Three, etc.) dramatize the absolute lack of communication between common people and institutions. Seeking to have his fourteen-year-old grandson released from service in the republic's galleys and restored to his care, the fisherman confronts his rulers with (for them) unacceptable notions of equality ("a fisherman hath his feelings as well as the doge" [74]), a denial of their power that is eventually — and ruthlessly — punished. Cooper's concern for the casualties of a profoundly unjust political system, his emphasis on the burden of the humble and the feeble (which may remind one, at times, of Manzoni's *The Betrothed*, first published in 1827), possibly contributed to the novel's popularity among contemporary Italian readers. Despite negative critical responses such as Zorzi's, the book's success was in fact considerable, as demonstrated by its going through four editions between 1835 and 1838. Although *The Bravo* was primarily intended as a cautionary tale for Americans, its description of totalitarianism could not but have a special resonance for the subjects of local and foreign tyrannies in

Risorgimento Italy. Cooper meant to exhort his countrymen to defend the liberty and justice that made the United States a republic true to its name, but no one could feel the force of his argument as much as those to whom liberty and justice were still denied. Notwithstanding its unrealistic aspects and its eighteenth-century setting, *The Bravo* might be read as a commentary (however indirect) on the political situation in nineteenth-century Italy.

Writing on *The Bravo* and other nineteenth-century texts, Rosella Mamoli Zorzi has noted that "in the case of the representations of Venice" in that period (and, to a certain extent, in this century as well) "the TEXT is the city, in the sense that the literary representation of Venice" is based "on *preexisting literary and visual representations* of Venice" (1990, 285). What I would like to suggest is that *for Italian readers of the 1830s,* the familiarity of the basic situation depicted in the book — roughly speaking, the absence of liberty — very likely outweighed the estranging artificiality of the context. If not in the character's traits, they could at least recognize themselves in their predicament. If the over-elaborate rhetoric and melodramatic temperament of a Jacopo or Antonio were foreign, the helplessness of these characters in the face of arbitrary laws was painfully known.

In his preface to *The Bravo*, Cooper made no mystery of the fact that his portrayal of the Venetian government was not the fruit of extensive historical research. Explaining that he had not attempted "to portray historical characters" but "simply to set forth the familiar operations of Venetian policy" (17), he openly identified his source as being Daru's *Histoire.* After all, Cooper's main aim in writing *The Bravo* was not to convincingly evoke the Venetian past. More than anything else, he wished to warn or, one is tempted to say, to frighten his American readers, confronting them with the possible involutions of a democratic system ("The author has endeavored to give *his countrymen* ... a picture of the social system of one of the *soi-disant* republics of the other hemisphere" [17, emphasis added]). Nevertheless, I think *The Bravo* may be read as a document of Cooper's Italian experience as much as can his nonfictional travel account *Gleanings in Europe: Italy.* Only in the latter, undeniably, does scrupulous observation prevail in the general representation of Italian customs, but it is in the novel that one finds echoes of the political climate of the country. Cooper intentionally ignored contemporary political reality in *Gleanings,* and that omission inevitably makes that work seem somewhat incomplete and, perhaps, also slightly insincere. It is in *The Bravo* that he suggested effectively the kind of political oppression he had had the opportunity of witnessing directly.


## Venetian Life

Howells's appointment as American consul in Venice, in 1861, came as a reward for writing a campaign biography of Lincoln the year before. Unlike Hawthorne, who had held the same position in Liverpool (1853–57), Howells soon discovered that, because of Venice's economic crisis and the scarce naval traffic of its port, his official duties were extremely limited and left him a considerable amount of time for study and writing. Except for the first three months of his sojourn (during which, because of bureaucratic delays, he was not officially authorized to act as consul and was not paid his salary), he was relatively free from major financial worries. Whereas in former times the remuneration for American consuls had been rather uncertain (in a port like Liverpool, it depended very much on fees from American shipping), in the years of Howells's appointment in Venice, the salary consisted of an annual stipend of $1,500. Howells was then able to devote his attention to the study of the Italian language and culture. Familiarity with the first opened the door to a new literary world (as demonstrated, in the years following, by numerous critical efforts, including "Recent Italian Comedy" [1864] and *Modern Italian Poets* [1887]). In particular, it made him discover the works of eighteenth-century Venetian dramatist Carlo Goldoni, whose brand of realism was to have a notable influence on his writing (especially on his theatrical production). Careful observation of local customs resulted in *Venetian Life*,[9] published in 1866, the year in which Venetia became part of the kingdom of Italy (a coincidence that contributed considerably to the book's fortune).

As Howells writes in the final section of the book, *Venetian Life* may be defined as an attempt to portray "another people's life and character"[10] (397). The author's study of local traits and living conditions is precise and detailed and indicates a commitment to actuality. He tries to replace the traditional literary image of a city dominated by a dark and insidious atmosphere with the quotidian aspect of no-longer-powerful, no-longer-wealthy nineteenth-century Venice. To use James L. Dean's phrase, Howells in *Venetian Life* shows "his awareness of ... the value of travel literature as a means of revelation and discovery" (1970, 9).

However, the author's purpose, as explained in the first chapter of his book, is also to argue that the real Venice — no matter how unlike the fantastic, gloomy place described by Byron, Cooper, and others — is still "to other cities like the pleasant improbability of the theatre to every-day, commonplace life" (10). It is an attempt, in other words, to remove the layer of illusions, for so long superimposed on the city, and bring to light its inherent, oneiric quality.

Not equally novel is the use of Venice, and Italy by extension, to define another society, another culture, for the economically stagnant and backward city depicted in *Venetian Life* helps to define dynamic and prosperous America as its contrasting model. At the same time, the dreamy, unreal quality of Venice — what makes it unlike any other place — emphasizes indirectly what in Howells's view is his country's major flaw: its excessively practical and concrete nature.

Both fantasy and reality enter Howells's ken as equally important and inseparable aspects of Venetian life. Common people in the streets and courts of the city may at once suggest mythic figures and illustrate the harsh actuality of poverty. Their physical features may intrigue the observer with the fancy that they are, perhaps, living pictures, but the reader is also reminded that their idleness is the consequence of a chronic lack of employment. Their aspect may be described as that of "saints and heroes ... madonnas and nymphs" (384), but we are not allowed to forget the hopelessness of their predicament. While implicitly stressing their figurative and exotic quality, the book does not overlook their primary identity: that of human beings faced with problems of an essentially economic character. A precarious compromise is reached between the point of view of the amateur artist and that of the sociologist.

The transfiguration of common humanity in *Venetian Life* is also to be considered in relation to the author's moral judgments. Throughout the book, Howells continuously imputes to the Italian character a lack of honesty and integrity — especially, though not exclusively, among the lower orders of society. The members of such classes, it would seem, are for the most part unworthy of any trust, marked as they are by a natural propensity for lying and cheating. Nevertheless, these very people do undergo, at times, a curious process through which they are idealized and, one might say, enveloped in myth. Idealization follows censure and vice versa, a phenomenon that has traditionally characterized the attitude of dominant social groups or cultures toward the "irrecoverable" (an exemplary American case is that of the Indians, as Roy Harvey Pearce has shown in *Savagism and Civilization,* 1988).

Observing an old man roasting coffee in a little court, Howells is fascinated with the personage's appearance, its arcane quality charmingly enhanced by the play of light and shadow caused by the fire in front of him. Strongly captivated by the spectacle, he speaks of the "grandeur" of "simple, abstract humanity" in Italy, and before our eyes transforms the old man into "some dread supernatural agency, turning the wheel of fortune" (35). Later in the book, he is once more struck by the appearance of another venerable character: the man he pays to clean his boat. Something in the man's face and gestures seems to transcend the actuality of his humble employment. So much so, indeed, that Howells does not hesitate to associate him with the figure of time and to reflect that he would be "much better occupied with an hourglass, or engaged with a scythe in mowing me and other mortals down" (114).

The author sees grandeur and timelessness in the same men and women he repeatedly typifies as knavish and honorless, but the two characterizations are not necessarily unreconcilable. They both suggest indistinctness and inscrutability and may be thought of as different faces of the same mystery. Whether Howells turns ordinary people into awesome personifications of fate or chastises them for their unreliability, his observations consistently imply complexity of character.

On reading Howells's account of his first impressions of Venice, one becomes aware of the fact that it is the quality of time that contributes mostly to what, to his eyes, is the city's strangeness. He finds himself surrounded by antiquity and decay, as present in buildings and monuments as in people's character and mores, and the impact could not be any greater for someone coming from "a land where everything, morally and materially" is "in good repair" (37). Time, moreover, not only impresses its visible and invisible marks upon the city and its inhabitants but also appears to hold its pace there and, occasionally, to halt altogether. It creates an atmosphere that, Howells believes, promotes indolence, that makes one lose touch with "the motion of the age" and the "wholesome struggle" (38) of active life. It creates a world in diametric opposition to the Protestant work ethic, a world where only those who possess strong will and "indomitable faith" can "retain ... a practical belief in God's purpose of a great moving, anxious, toiling, aspiring world outside" (38).

Life in Venice, as it is at times described in the book, is characterized by such a slow rhythm that, the author implies, it resembles a perennial slumber. The typical winter evenings of Venetian men, spent for the most part sitting at a café smoking, drinking coffee, reading, or playing chess, seem to Howells to be "torpid ... lifeless ... and intolerable" when compared to "the bright, social winter evenings of another and happier land and civilization" (43). However, one is also confronted with passages in which the faster tempo and more active character of American life is less fondly remembered and is certainly not equated with happiness. It is with amusement, but also, I think, a measure of embarrassment, that Howells reports, in chapter 13, the story of a "sharp, bustling, go-ahead Yankee" arriving one day on the island of the Armenians (San Lazzaro), "rubbing his hands" and asking the monks, "Show me all you can in five minutes" (197).

By drawing our attention to the quality of time in Italy, Howells indirectly suggests one of the main reasons for the presence of the American artist in the country. His words seem in fact to betray a fascination with the idea of taking the time to live, to do things that, while having no practical usefulness or value, are perhaps the ones that nourish and sustain us through our existence. And Venice offers him countless examples of this concept of time — one might term it the denial of modernity — equally notable in people's manners as in their trades. It is possible to identify it, for instance, in the prodigious patience of goldsmiths, weavers, and other artisans or, perhaps, in the ancient tradition of mosaic painting. Looking at the lower orders of labor, it may be recognized in the lack of mechanization and practicality, and the laborious, old-fashioned character of working methods.

> [They] work in old-world, awkward, picturesque ways, and not in commonplace, handy, modern fashion. Neither the habits nor the implements of labor are changed since the progress of the Republic ceased.... All sorts of mechanics' tools are clumsy and inconvenient.... [D]oor-hinges are made to order.... [A]ll nails and tacks are hand-made.... [Y]ou do not buy a door-lock at a hardware store, — you get a *fabbro* to make it. (340–41)

When he comments on the ceremonious urbanity of Venetians, the number of elaborate compliments they exchange on various occasions, he suggests that, however charming, such customs are often unaccompanied by sincerity and virtue. American bluntness, on the contrary, is seen as symptomatic of simpler and sounder ethics, and hence is preferable. However, although Howells's view on the subject appears to parallel that of Hawthorne in *The Marble Faun*, one can hardly fail to notice a greater degree of uncertainty in the author of *Venetian Life*.

> It is this uncostly gentleness of bearing which gives a winning impression of the whole people, whatever selfishness or real discourtesy lie beneath it. At home it sometimes seem that we are in such haste to live and be done with it, we have no time to be polite. Or is popular politeness merely a vice of servile peoples? And is it altogether better to be rude? I wish it were not. (352)

Writing on local character traits, Howells notes at some point that the ways of the Italian people are "childlike and simple in many things" (340), an observation difficult to reconcile with the prevailing tone of the rest of the book. In the city he describes, deception seems to be practiced at all levels of society, from the petty frauds of servants and peddlers to the highly sophisticated scheming of the high bourgeoisie. Lying, we are told, is cultivated as little less than an art form, and people of both sexes and all ages seem to have a natural disposition and an enormous talent for it. It is of slyness and duplicity, rather than of naïveté, that Howells repeatedly offers us examples, his tone varying from the amused to the indignant, but with a clear prevalence of the latter.

Telling of the days in which Venice was at its most powerful, he devotes particular attention to the shrewd, unscrupulous character of Venetian commerce. The Venetians, he points out, were of all people "the most deeply involved" (239) in the slave trade and conducted it in the most ingenious and unprincipled of manners. Howells does not confront, however, one of the most fascinating questions concerning the central role of commerce in the republic's history: how, that is, this utter devotion to business, apparently symptomatic of a culture where materialism and philistinism dominated, could coexist with an extraordinary flourishing of the arts. Instead, he chooses to concentrate on the state's inexorable decline, as the original enterprising spirit gradually gave way to luxury and indolence, and he reads the fall of the republic as a stern moral lesson (254–57). His great concern with ethics is again confirmed when he sums up his impression of the moral fiber of the present population in the final part of the book. Referring to what he calls the common view of Italians as fundamentally dishonest, Howells explains how his personal experience has both confirmed and disproved such an opinion. The student of Italian character should not forget, he reminds us, the figure of Garibaldi, the hero whose uncommon valor and love of truth are sufficient evidence that his "race" cannot be branded as one of "liars and cheats" (361). Nor should one fail to consider, as a justification of many flaws, the pernicious influence of "long ages of alien and domestic oppression, in politics and religion" (361). However, Howells concludes:

> after exception and palliation has been duly made, it must be confessed that in Italy it does not seem to be thought shameful to tell lies, and that there the standard of sincerity, compared with that of the English or American, is low, as the Italian standard of morality in other respects is also comparatively low. (361)

Severity prevails likewise on the subject of religion, which Howells often relates to art. Unlike Hawthorne, Howells does not maintain that Catholicism may have originated directly from paganism, but rather that it has become the heir of that worship in its modern and corrupt state. He does refer, at times, to the pristine spiritual vigor of the Catholic faith: he recognizes it, for instance, in the beauty of St. Mark's Church. Like St. Peter's in *The Marble Faun* and *The Italian Sketch Book*, St. Mark's, at once reassuring and awe inspiring, is presented as a house for all faiths. Still, in Howells's final analysis, the exemplification of modern Catholicism is not to be found in St. Mark's but rather in the many Renaissance churches of the city. Their architecture and decorations, for which he repeatedly expresses a violent dislike (in line with Ruskin's teachings, of which he was a devout follower), appear to Howells to bespeak the soullessness and superstition that have taken the place of the early faith. In their cold marbles he reads the death of authentic religious feeling; they are, in his words:

> fit tabernacles for that droning and mumming spirit which has deprived all young and generous men in Italy of religion; which has made the priests a bitter jest and byword; which has rendered the population ignorant, vicious, and hopeless. (161)

The reader of *Venetian Life*, unlike the reader of *The Marble Faun*, can have no doubt that the city described in the book is under foreign rule, as the question is confronted from the very first chapter. Howells comments in fact on the population's fierce hostility toward the occupying regime, and one detects a somehow unexpected element of surprise in his tone, as he observes that the hatred of Austria is "marvelously unanimous and bitter" (17). His point of view, at this stage, is quite different from that of Margaret Fuller and Julia Ward Howe who, as we have seen, respond intensely to the French occupation of Rome and seem to regard their "Americanness" as leaving them no choice but to support the struggle for self-government. But Howells, recently arrived in Venice, does not seem aware of a possible parallel between the local movement for independence and the revolutionary past of his own nation. What he expresses in these first pages is not an interest in analyzing the source of the political tension around him but rather a feeling of vexation at finding himself in a city drastically divided into two camps. His concern seems to be limited to the extent to which the situation affects an external observer such as he. In his words: "the annoyance which it gives the foreigner might well damp any passion with which he was disposed to speak of its cause" (17).

Admittedly, the diplomatic character of Howells's official appointment helps to explain the viewpoint of his preoccupations. One can readily imagine the difficulty of functioning in a city in which association of any kind with the ruling power meant the enmity of the local population and one's exclusion from their society. Yet, the way in which he approaches and phrases the issue seems almost to suggest a view of Venetian libertarian aspirations as somewhat preposterous; they are the aspirations of a people "*believing* themselves born for freedom and independence" (19; emphasis added).

It is certainly with a different spirit that, later in the book, Howells denounces the church for its support of despotism (as Cooper also does in *The Bravo*). He seems to echo Fuller when, looking back at the days of the old Venetian republic, he speaks of the "priceless rights" (258) of which the people were then deprived, when the government promoted artificial merriment through a seemingly endless series of festivals and holidays to compensate for the absence of real freedom — or, when he comments unfavorably on the tendency, among the lower classes, to expect improvement of their conditions as the result of a gracious concession from above, rather than as the recognition of an inalienable, God-given right. It is in moments like these that Howells insists on what is clearly a basic democratic principle: the connection between human dignity and freedom — a dignity which, he significantly points out, has already been partially achieved in the independent part of Italy.

In chapter after chapter, one senses in Howells's remarks on politics and social conditions an increasing urgency and emotional participation that contrasts sharply with his initial cautiousness and detachment. Noteworthy are, in this sense, his views on the interrelation of different levels of society in Italy. He calls the reader's attention to the urbanity and "free and unembarrassed bearing of all ranks of people toward each other" (382) as opposed to the marked sense of social difference recognizable in the life of other European countries, and the brutal "distinction of rich and poor" that one sometimes witnesses in America's "*soi-disant* democratic society" (382). It is a sense of equality that he believes to be deeply rooted in the "Italian fibre" and that, in his words, "fits the nation for democratic institutions better than any other" (382).

In the first part of the book one senses Howells's disappointment as he tells of the mournful character of the city,[11] with its scarce and languid social life and the effects of the anti-Austrian "demonstration," which kept most of the population from attending the opera. In the end, he has only words of praise for the city's demeanor, for what he describes as the "sacrifice of all that makes life easy and joyous, to the attainment of a good which shall make life noble" (398). It is hardly accidental, I believe, that the shift in Howells's attitude in the second half of *Venetian Life* is accompanied by more frequent references to the life and manners of his native country. It is as if the recurring thought of liberties and privileges he had formerly taken for granted gave him new empathic insight into the predicament of the Venetians. The impression is that his greater appreciation of this foreign land, his learning more of its ways and people, gives him a profounder understanding of his own nation and the principles on which it was founded. It is with new democratic fervor that he devotes his final considerations to the people whose ambitions of independence he had, perhaps, previously undervalued.

The Venetians desire now, and first of all things, Liberty, knowing that in slavery men can learn no virtues; and I think them fit, with all their errors and defects, to be free now, because men are never fit to be slaves. (398)

# 4

## Forgotten Voices:
## Henry T. Tuckerman's
## *The Italian Sketch Book* (1835)
## and Henry P. Leland's
## *Americans in Rome* (1863)

As early as the first decades of the nineteenth century, the author of "yet another" account of an Italian journey reassured his readers that what awaited them was not — or, at least, not only — a perfunctory description of standardized episodes (a moonlit ramble in the Coliseum, St. Peter's, the Uffizi, the Bridge of Sighs, etc.).

The need to distinguish one's rendering of the "Italian experience" sometimes resulted in a preference for the quotidian, the ordinary aspects of the country, over its artistic patrimony. Quite a few in fact were those writers who thought the task of translating into words the aesthetic impact of art works not merely difficult but fruitless.

For an American author, the choice of placing greater emphasis on the study of humanity than on the study of art could also be motivated by a specific interest in comparative analysis. If one wished to establish a cultural contrast between the United States and Italy, it was undoubtedly less difficult to examine and compare different manners and mentalities than to choose the American counterparts of Michelangelo's *Moses* or Guido Reni's *Beatrice Cenci*.

Both works examined in this chapter — Henry T. Tuckerman's *The Italian Sketch Book* (1835) and Henry P. Leland's *Americans in Rome*

(1863) — are representative of such an anthropological bent. In presenting his volume to the readers, Tuckerman describes it as a collection of tales and essays "illustrative of the local and social features"[1] of Italy. Its purpose, he furthermore informs us, is that of awakening "in any mind an interest and faith in humanity as there existent" (vii). Humanity is also the main subject in *Americans in Rome.* Leland notes in his preface that whereas pages and pages have been written on the "antiquities" of Rome, little attention has been devoted to the city's "popular and genial life" (3).[2]

The introductory parts of the two books stress the instructive value of an encounter with Italian culture. Its antiquity, its difference, are indicated as the measure by which American travelers or readers can outline the conditions, merits, or deficiencies of their own society. In the very first pages of their works, both Tuckerman and Leland identify their interlocutors and address them in a plainly didactic tone; but a great difference is soon revealed. Tuckerman warns his readers that a certain degree of intellectual preparation is indispensable to the kind of research proposed in the *Sketch Book.* Italian reality, in his view, does not yield itself passively to one's gaze, nor is the task made easier by the "long and magnifying space which divides ... [the American] continent from the old world." Precious for the "transatlantic sojourner in Italy" are "a sense of the true nature of the comprehensive object" she or he is "about to contemplate," "a patient determination to bestow a degree of time and study in a measure corresponding with the subject, a preparedness for disappointment, and an unyielding spirit of candor." As conceived by Tuckerman, travel is a discipline complete with a body of specific "methods" (ix–x).

For Leland, on the other hand, the major question is not so much "how" an American should look at Italy as "why." What is the benefit of an immersion in the past — for such is the experience of Rome — for a people who with "their war[3] and work, are fighting along stoutly in the advance guard of the world"? The answer lies in Leland's definition of Rome as America's "antithesis" (3; these words recall Charles Eliot Norton's view in the 1859 *Notes of Travel and Study in Italy*, 163–64). It is Rome's alien quality that renders it the ideal reference point against which the achievements of the New World can be appraised. Its antiquity which, Leland points out, is not only made of ruins and relics but also informs the habits, rituals, and gestures of its people, can help one comprehend and appreciate America's modernity. The city's "otherness" makes it function, in relation to America, as an "image seen in a looking glass" (Lévi-Strauss 1964, 138).

### The Italian Sketch Book

Like several other nineteenth-century travelers, Henry T. Tuckerman went to Italy hoping that his health would benefit from the country's renowned mildness of climate. In that he was disappointed. Italy failed to correspond to the romantic image of a land unvisited by the asperities of winter. What he found instead was a "vocation." His first Italian sojourn — from October to March of 1833, mostly in Florence and Rome — brought him, in his early twenties, to undertake a career as a writer. His impressions of Italy were first recorded in articles and tales that appeared in *The Boston Pearl and Literary Gazette* in 1834. The following year a few of these pieces and additional materials were published as a book with the title *The Italian Sketch Book* (an evident reference to Irving's own *Sketch Book* [1820], whose composite form Tuckerman imitated).

Tuckerman's literary production was evidently affected by his contact with Italy. After the *Sketch Book* came *Isabel, or Sicily* (1839) and *Rambles and Reveries* (1841), both inspired by his second trip to the peninsula (1836–38); moreover, a great many of his subsequent works concern or include references to, Italy.

Unlike better-known and more widely studied American representations of Italy such as *The Marble Faun* and *Venetian Life*, the *Sketch Book* is scarcely characterized by judgments of a moral kind. This is made evident, for example, by Tuckerman's treatment of the themes of art and religion, two aspects of Italian life of particularly difficult interpretation for most Protestant observers. What emerges from Tuckerman's comments on churches, monuments, and art galleries is a capacity for simple aesthetic pleasure apparently inconceivable to most American writers of his time.

Exemplary in this sense is the account of his visits to St. Peter's, where it was his "special delight" to go "not critically to examine, but to yield [himself] freely to its sublimity and beauty" (21). In admiring the colossal architectural structure of St. Peter's, Tuckerman unhesitatingly identifies its double significance: (1) as a symbol of man's capacity for excellence ("there is a freedom, a nobleness, a grandeur about St. Peter's, allied to intellect and sentiment in their higher manifestations" [22]), and (2) as a place of worship ("the thought of that Being to whose praises it is devoted"[22]). What ultimately prevails, however, in his intellectual and emotional response to St. Peter's, is an essentially secular appreciation of beauty. To the eyes of most American authors in Italy, the religious and aesthetic values of Catholic churches appear inseparable: the admiration of the first brings a sense of guilt, as if it were an implicit approbation of the latter. In Tuckerman's case, on the contrary, the fact that St. Peter's is a place "dedicated to Catholicism" (23) is somewhat secondary to its being "a magnificent edifice," and it does not interfere with the observer's "calm sentiment of satisfaction" (22).

Even those manifestations of Catholic worship which usually struck a Protestant visitor as exceedingly peculiar and theatrical are commented on in the *Sketch Book* in a remarkably detached tone. Telling of his visit to the Church of the Capuchins and its cemetery, Tuckerman concentrates mainly on visual details. Monastic life interests him but remains something very far from his experience. The reader's impression is that Tuckerman's awareness of this "distance" is what causes a suspension of judgment on his part. The spectacle of the cemetery, with its stretched skeletons and its lamps made of bones, is defined as "hideous" (26), but Tuckerman's tone throughout the description is surprisingly matter-of-fact. The contrast could not be greater, with the triumph of horrific detail and moral indignation that characterizes the same scene in *The Marble Faun* (chaps. 20–21).

Also noteworthy are the accounts of a ceremony for the entrance of two young women into the novitiate[4] and a religious procession in the town of Prato. Like Margaret Fuller, Tuckerman shows a taste for the poetic and pictorial character of Catholic liturgy (the novitiates' "interesting appearance, and the associations of the moment, were not inoperative upon those of us to whom the scene was new" [45]). What distinguishes his attitude, though, is a reluctance to pronounce himself on the sincerity of the rituals he witnesses, on whether or not their spirituality equals their suggestiveness. To recognize something as different from what we know, Tuckerman seems to suggest, means to defer the evaluation of "what is better, [or] morally sounder" (Hildegard Eilert 1989, 65). As refers, specifically, to the forms and expressions of worship, Tuckerman focuses on their comprehensive effect, the sensation that they

communicate to the observer. His insistence on the novelty of the scenes
he is contemplating is hardly accidental.

> As this was the first ceremonial of the kind I had witnessed, my interest was
> considerably excited.... The combined effect of such a solemn moving
> pageant, and the gazing multitude ... the profound stillness which reigned ...
> the deep tones of the chanters, or the measured strains of the instruments ...
> all came most touchingly and with an awful and solemn distinctness upon the
> mind. (69–70)

In his study of travel literature, Percy Adams draws a parallel between
fictional heroes and travelers/narrators. Just as the fictional character
"controls the fictional narrative, moves through space, and grows with
that movement or is exposed by it, so ... does many a" traveler/narrator
"control the account or move, grow, become exposed in it" (1983, 185).
For both, the movement through space and time can assume the characteristics of an education, or an apprenticeship. If such is the case, an
intellectual course may be detected and followed as it unwinds alongside
the geographical one.

To be sure, there is in Tuckerman's *Sketch Book* a cultural trajectory
that is not represented by the passage from city to city, region to region.
Tuckerman's discovery and interpretation of Italian life is also a discovery and interpretation of the role of author. Writing on Roman ruins, he
emphasizes the creative effort involved in the act of beholding them (a
concept also formulated by Melville in his 1857 lecture on "Statues in
Rome" [1987, 404]). Their obscurity, their remoteness, allow the
observer to supply with his or her imagination what time has canceled
("free scope is ... given to a species of conjecture, which it is mournfully
pleasing to indulge" [34]). Not surprisingly, the inscription on the tomb
of Cecilia Metella fascinates Tuckerman because of its "sublime simplicity"; the scanty information it provides makes it appealing, for it is very
much like the first sentence of a tale or a novel yet to be written.

> Standing by the massive remains of such a mausoleum, of which we can only
> affirm that it was reared to the memory of a Roman wife and daughter —
> what trait of energetic beauty, of affectionate devotion, of moral courage,
> which enters into the *beau-ideal* of the female character, may we not
> confidently ascribe to this? (34)

As a person without a history, a person defined only by her domestic and social roles or functions (wife and daughter), Cecilia Metella becomes in the *Sketch Book* the emblem of woman in any time and place. Cecilia's mausoleum (dismissed in Cooper's *Gleanings in Europe: Italy* as a monument to "insignificance" [1981, 206]) is for Tuckerman an appropriate symbol for the unheard history of "innumerable of her sex." We are likely to think of Thomas Gray and George Eliot as we follow Tuckerman's reflections on the women who

> live in the exercise of thoughts and sentiments which, if developed through more conspicuous channels, would be productive of deathless renown; but whose self-sacrificing ministrations, though immeasurably influential, are as unseen as those of a guardian angel. (35)

The terms in which Tuckerman sets up a contrast between the cultural identities of Italy and the United States seem to betray reservations about certain aspects of modernity. The underlying suggestion of quite a few passages of the *Sketch Book* appears to be that there are human qualities whose growth is particularly favored by a preindustrial environment. Interestingly enough, similar theories also make their appearance, in the same period, in Italy's internal debate over the definition of the country's national essence. A highly emphatic and self-righteous version of Tuckerman's contraposition of sentiment and practicality may be found, for example, in one of the most popular works of the Risorgimento: Vincenzo Gioberti's *Del Primato morale e civile degli Italiani* [Of the civil and moral supremacy of Italians] (1843). Replacing America as nation-symbol of modernity is, in *Del Primato,* her closest European equivalent: England. The citizens of such a thriving, advanced nation have apparently a very strong claim to the title of first people in the world, and yet, Gioberti argues, they are inferior to the Italians. What determines this inferiority is, apart from the fact that they are not Catholic, the excessive emphasis that their society places upon the material sphere of existence (1846, 2:386, 389, 166).

An attempt to define the Italian nature as naturally at odds with aggressive utilitarianism and competitiveness comes also from Gioberti's chief political rival, Mazzini, in his *Dei doveri dell'uomo* [Of the duties of man] (1845). As Bollati has observed, Mazzini's search for a "more humane" Italian model of modernity played an important role in creating the popular image of the "good, brotherly" Italian incapable of "ruthless aggressiveness" (1989, 1011). This is an image not dissimilar to that evoked by Tuckerman in the section of his book called "The Last Sojourn."

> I felt that if the social activity and predominance of mental endeavor which characterize my own country were wanting here, yet that I had known and experienced much of the true spirit of fraternity, much of intellectual enthusiasm and generous sentiment. I thought of the many hours of quiet and innocent enjoyment, the instances of social kindness, the offices of sympathy. (123–24)

The concept of "fraternity" (which, as we have seen, is also stressed by Fuller and Howe) may be viewed in Tuckerman as closely related to that of communication, of mutual comprehension. It is well to remember that Tuckerman's knowledge of Italian allowed him not only to establish a dialogue with the people he wished to portray but also to recreate their voice on the page. "Society," in Talal Asad's phrase, is "people who speak" (1986, 155), and understanding their speech is the key to understanding their society. What a foreign language stands for is not only a different lexicon, a different grammar, but also, and more importantly, a different way of thinking, a different way of confronting the world. Using the local language (with which, as he points out in the *Sketch Book*, he was adequately but not fully acquainted), Tuckerman in Italy accepted a position of vulnerability that most travelers in his time did their best to avoid. He managed, at times, to abandon the role of spectator by putting himself in the middle of things, interacting with the people he described.

When observing the Italian scene from within, rather than from without, Tuckerman sees things in a different way. The amiable generalizations that characterize some of his descriptions of the Italian character (especially in the tales "The Florentine" and "The Sad Bird of the Adriatic," as well as in the section entitled "Natural Language") are replaced by vivid sketches of believable individuals. Though not displaying the proverbial "sanguinary temperament" (53) and "ardor" (221), nor doing justice to their description as "children of feeling" (264), Tuckerman's few Italian acquaintances are among the most interesting figures in the *Sketch Book*. The account of his encounter with a young Sicilian poet in Naples serves, for instance, as a rare and revealing illustration of one of the Italian images of the New World. Two simple words pronounced by Tuckerman, "*Sono Americano*," open up vistas of unlimited expression and liberty ("his eye brightened.... He spoke enthusiastically of Washington and Franklin" [90]). As an author, the young man is particularly interested in "the extent of the liberty of the press in America"; when Tuckerman tells him of the situation in that country, he experiences both elation and despair. The image evoked by Tuckerman's words is enormously appealing, the contrast with his own predicament far too sharp ("He struck his hand despondingly upon a pile of manuscripts, the publication of which the censors had prohibited, on the ground of their liberty of sentiment" [90–91]). The faceless mass of the victims of oppression finds in this episode a recognizable voice, a specific identity. Tuckerman thus succeeds in presenting the direct effects of despotism, a reality otherwise difficult to visualize for his American readers.

In the section entitled "My Home Abroad," Tuckerman notes how a sojourner's experience of a foreign land depends on "the position whence" he "gazes forth." If he associates with the local population, if he lives with them, his apprehension of "external nature," his "impressions of social and moral phenomena" will differ greatly from those of "the wanderer who looks forth from his own solitary consciousness" (230). These observations (suggesting almost an early description of anthropological fieldwork) introduce Tuckerman's recollection of his stay in Florence and the special quality of his relationship with his two landladies (a mature countess and her daughter). As in the former episode, Tuckerman gives us here a glimpse of America as filtered through an Italian sensitivity; once more, the emphasis is on the mythical connotation of the word "American":

> Her [the countess's] early and affectionate interest in me was at first unaccountable, until I learned the romantic sentiments with which the very name of American was associated in her mind. Her ideas on this subject were derived, in no small degree, from the novels of the *Seconda Valter Scott* (sic), as she called Cooper, the translations of which she had eagerly pondered. (233)

Tuckerman's avowed interest in humanity is an expression of his attitude toward the interrelation of past and present in Italy. Unlike many other travelers, Tuckerman finds the country's contemporary scene as engrossing as the remnants and traces of history. There are times when modern Italy, with its political and social questions and its various cultural expressions[5] seems to absorb completely the author's attention.

Whereas Hawthorne and Howells, as we have seen, view the presence of the past in Italy as overwhelming (to the point that it renders the present evanescent and dream-like), Tuckerman emphasizes the immediacy of the present, the force of its impact on the viewer.

Often, in the *Sketch Book,* a parallel study of Italy's past and present is indicated as the best strategy for an analysis of the country's complex nature. Only looking back at Italy's history can the foreign visitor understand its many divisions, the texture of a country where the "us versus them" clash multiplies and fragments in a series of subcategories (region versus region, city versus city, village versus village, neighborhood versus neighborhood). Only by considering how a long succession of foreign invasions has in the course of the centuries "neutralized her nationality" may one venture to discuss "the present moral and social condition of Italy" (266). The would-be visitors of Italy whom Tuckerman ideally addresses are constantly reminded that their intellectual gain will depend on the quality of their effort. They must be aware that "of all countries [Italy] requires special study, and calm habitual attention, to develop its resources" (75). The American, the citizen of "the active, the bustling world" must acquire a different mentality to conform to and appreciate the "contemplative spirit" of the country. The mechanical movement from place to place, the incessant search for new objects, new scenes, that characterizes fashionable travel, is in Tuckerman's view "singularly inconsistent" (75) with the character of the land. It represents a violation of the local culture, an intrusion of values that are antithetical to it. Based as it is on respect, Tuckerman's own way to relate to another reality is the very opposite of violence. Only respect, Tuckerman suggests in the *Sketch Book*, favors a constructive exploration of diversity and, consequently, the acquisition of wisdom.

### *Americans in Rome*

In chapter 2 of *Americans in Rome* (originally serialized in the *Continental Monthly* in 1862–63 as *Macaroni and Canvas*), the painters Rocjan and Caper decide to play a joke on the latter's uncle, Mr. William Brown of St. Louis, who had recently arrived in Europe. They tell him that they will accompany him to a grand ball given by the Prince Nicolo (sic) di Giacinti, a ball that will be attended by the best Roman nobility.

Once there, Mr. Brown is pleasantly surprised by the enormous affability and good-naturedness of the illustrious guests. Apparently, they enjoy nothing more than drinking large quantities of red wine and dancing energetically in brightly colored costumes. As it turns out, the men and women introduced to Mr. Brown as princes, princesses, marquises, and countesses are not the real thing. As Caper reveals to his uncle the morning after the party, the people with whom they drank and danced were actually models: members of the lower classes who, for a fee, turn themselves into aristocrats, gladiators, shepherds, or whatever is required by the artist who hires them.

For the Italian reader of *Americans in Rome* (who is doubtlessly not the author's intended interlocutor), it is as if that ball did not end with the close of the chapter. The scenes of Roman life described in the book (on the basis of true incidents, as the author points out in the preface, [4]) often give the impression of being inhabited by performers rather than by ordinary individuals. It may be hard to reconcile such a theatrical effect with the terms in which Leland describes his work, with its being "almost to the minutest details true in spirit," because the fruit of "observation" (4).

The difference between intentions and results, however, appears less marked if one focuses on Leland's specific definition of his field of investigation. Leland informs us, in the same preface, that during his stay in Rome and its surroundings (between the fall of 1857 and that of 1858), he noted down "carefully many curious characteristics of popular life and humor" (4). The word "curious" defines the author's gaze as selective. We may assume that in portraying Rome's popular life, he illuminated peculiarity and quaintness rather than ordinariness. Interestingly enough, the characters chosen as representative of that life are not only "natives" but also "strangers who adapted themselves to native customs" (4). The gallery of grotesques (for such are most of Leland's creations) that one encounters in *Americans in Rome* is indeed composed as much of Italians as of citizens of several European countries, and of course, the United States. But Leland's reference to a phenomenon of adaptation to local customs is slightly misleading. It may appear to suggest that the peculiarity of certain characters is the result of their Roman sojourn (they have "absorbed" the otherness of Rome). Quite to the contrary, national traits in *Americans in Rome* are seen as intensified and brought into bold relief by the atmosphere of the city.

With its insistence on seriousness of method and instructive purpose, the author's preface to *Americans in Rome* "hardly prepares" for the "irreverent" book that follows (Vance 1990, 2:147). Anticipating Mark Twain's *The Innocents Abroad* (1869), Leland's novel subverts in fact some of the most solid conventions of travel books on Italy. To be explored in the novel is not, for a change, the significance of an artistic pilgrimage but rather the satiric potential of a foreigner's immersion into Italian life. In the very first chapter, we discover, for instance, that although James Caper, the protagonist and fictional alter ego of the author, is an artist, art is by no means his chief concern in Rome.

> "My mission in this great city is not that of a picture peddler or art student. I come to investigate the eating, drinking, sleeping arrangements of the Eternal City — its wine more than its vinegar, its pretty girls more than its galleries, its cafés more than its churches." (12–13)

The same is also true of Caper's closest friend and colleague, Rocjan (an "Americanized" Frenchman, having lived in Boston for several years), as well as, in general, of the whole artistic community of Rome. Doubtless, we are very far from the traditional figure of the artist visiting Italy in search of inspiration, of direct contact with the works of the masters. As in chapter 15 ("An Æsthetic Company") of *The Marble Faun*, the target of the author's satire in *Americans in Rome* is the romantic aura of spirituality and purity that is part of that characterization. If Hawthorne subtly undermines that image, commenting on the banal human faults of painters and sculptors (petty jealousies and rivalries in glaring contrast to their "noble" vocation), Leland destroys it altogether by showing his characters as chiefly absorbed by the most prosaic aspects of life.

Even the very meaning and function of traditional forms of art are called into question in the novel. The author has Rocjan theorize, at some point, the superiority of useful, practical objects over what is represented on canvas or in marble. The way Rocjan phrases his argument, stressing the relation between form and function, echoes the mid-nineteenth-century debate over the organic principle in art. In particular, we are reminded of Horatio Greenough's views on "functional beauty," of his conviction that those objects are beautiful whose structure is the result of an adaptation to the needs of ordinary life.[6]

Art, applied solely to sculpture and painting, is dead; it will not rise again in these our times. But art, the fairy-fingered beautifier of all that surrounds our homes and daily walks, save paintings and statuary, never breathed so fully, clearly, nobly, as now.... The rough-handed artisan, who, slowly dreaming of the beautiful, at last turns out a stove that will beautify and adorn a room, instead of rendering it hideous, has done for this practical generation what he of an earlier theoretical age did for his contemporaries, when he carved the imperial Venus of Milos. (40)

To claim the status of art for the production of household equipment is, of course, primarily a way to ennoble a field in which America is felt to be in the forefront, to have the advantage over Europe. The fact that this expression of faith in the possibilities of modernity (and of its symbol: The Unites States) is pronounced by Rocjan is hardly casual. As is the case throughout the novel, it is the European who has for a long time experienced America (and who is then best qualified to compare the two ways of life) who more or less explicitly suggests that the future belongs to the New World.

Through Rocjan's speeches, the author is able to abandon at times the mode of comedy to introduce a series of reflections on his country. On such occasions, American readers are exhorted to consider the achievements of their nation in relation to the present and past history of Europe. The political predicament of Italy, in particular, is viewed as full of lessons for the citizens of a democracy born from a fierce struggle for independence. What is mainly emphasized is the privileged condition of America ("the only really blessed and happy nation in the world"), something of which its people do not seem sufficiently aware ("your educated men know less of the history of their own country, and feel less its sublime teachings, than any other race of men in the world" [52]). As in Julia Ward Howe's poem "A Protest from Italy," one detects in Leland's novel a concern for the country's immaturity. The references to the Civil War ("the sermon will be preached by the god of battles to the roar of cannons and the crack of rifles, and I hope you'll profit by it after you hear it" [53]), for example, indicate a view of this event as an almost welcomed rite of initiation, marking America's entrance into adulthood.

Like Margaret Fuller, Leland on more than one occasion exhorts his readers to learn more about themselves; he differs, however, from the author of *Woman in the Nineteenth Century* in equating America's self-knowledge with a recognition of greatness. Fuller's previously mentioned

remark that "the American in Europe, if a thinking mind, can only become more American" (250) assured her public that the study of foreign
cultures did not involve a loss of identity and was meant as a critique of
the arrogant self-satisfaction of some of her countrymen. Starting from
the same premise, Leland gives his own alternative formula: "the advantages of foreign travel to an intelligent American are to teach him ... the
disadvantages of living anywhere save in America" (124).

It is a lesson which, the novel suggests, may be fully inferred through
a careful study of the visual impact of things. A comparison between
Italian and American urban landscapes is only apparently destined to be
unfavorable to the latter. Undeniably, Leland observes, the "artistic eye"
is better pleased by the "soothing colors of Italy ... the subdued white
and gray tones of Roman ruins and palaces, walls and houses" than by
the "fiery-red bricks" (124) of American cities. But the evaluation of a
landscape should not be based solely on aesthetic designations. What
Leland indicates is an idea of the landscape as a system of signs, as a
field in which it is possible to analyze "man, his activities, his entire
cultural world" (Turri 1983, 74). The plainness and simplicity of American dwellings is then an expression of sincerity, honesty, and determination. Their aspect does not distract from the exercise of duty, from the
demanding rhythm of daily toil. Rather, their brutal, offensive color
"goads [the American] on, as it doth a bull, to make valorous efforts —
to do something!" (124).

In exercising his creativity, Leland's American artist privileges functionality and commercial sense over beauty. It is perfectly legitimate for
him to think of his activity as a form of business, provided he is straight-
forward about it. On the side of the "good" are Caper, Rocjan, and those
of their colleagues who, with great satisfaction of the eminently practical
and philistine Mr. Browne, never mention the word "art." ("If I didn't
know I was with artists in Rome ... I should think I was among a lot of
smart merchants.... I feel at home with you" [113]). What is condemned
in *Americans in Rome* is instead the hypocrisy of those who hide that
same commercial sense behind a façade of pretentiousness. Thus, the
closest thing to a villain in the novel is the American sculptor Chapin,
always citing the rules of art and, at the same time, searching for new
ways to accelerate his production of statuary. William Vance has
suggested that this character may have been modeled on the sculptors
Hiram Powers and Randolph Rogers (1990, 1:211).

"Them were splendid old fellows, them Greeks. There was art for you —
high art! ... They worked for a precious few; but we do it up for the many.
Now, there's the A-poller Belvidiary — beautiful thing; but the idea of
brushin' his hair that way is ridicoolus.... They had a way among the Greeks
of fixing their drapery right well; but I've invented a plan — for which I've
applied to Washington for a patent — that I think will beat anything Phidias
ever did." (36–37)

As I pointed out in the Introduction, the average American traveler in
nineteenth-century Italy had but brief and insignificant contacts with the
local population. In part for lack of interest, in part because of the logis-
tics of travel, the traveler's experience was mostly limited to the lower
orders of society (what Tuckerman possibly refers to as "the extreme
exemplars of the population" [263]). In Leland's case, though, the association with those social strata was not accidental but rather eagerly
sought. They represented his chosen — and, one might add, his only —
subject of study. His assertion in the preface to *Americans in Rome* that
he had "constantly born in mind the variety of elements in Roman
society" (4) is clearly contradicted by the text. What he does in the novel
is actually to portray only one section of that society, indicating it as
representative of the local — and even the national — character. As a
result, the contrast with American life proposed in the book is frequently
unbalanced. A significant example is provided by a scene in chapter 4, in
which Caper, Rocjan, and their English friend Bagswell socialize with a
group of country people at a Roman inn. Leland calls our attention to the
three women who are part of the company and who are just as lively and
fun loving as the men.

Conversation then fell on the fair; and one of the Italians told several stories
which were broad enough to have shoved the generality of English and American ladies out of the window of the room. But Angeluccia and the two wives
of the stout gentlemen never winked; they had probably been to confession
that morning, had cleared out their old sins, and were now ready to take in a
new cargo. (81)

Having duly noticed the author's final comments on religion (a sort of
milder, more tolerant version of Hawthorne's ideas on the "convenience"
of Catholicism), it is well to focus on the transverse character of the
comparison, for the manners of uneducated peasant women are not

placed side by side with those of their American social equivalent. Implicitly, I believe, the readers are invited to identify the second term of comparison (English and American ladies) as representative of their same (supposedly) genteel, middle-class standards. Ignoring any kind of class consideration, Leland opts for a hasty, inaccurate translation of social terms.

Leland's identification of the Italian character with plebeian traits and manners is not to be viewed, however, as solely aimed at encouraging a condescending bias in his readers, for behind that choice there is also, in a sense, a desire to be anthropologically correct. The customs of the Roman lower classes are in fact indicated in the novel as the most authentic, the least affected by foreign influences. As Leland often points out, they may still be observed with the assurance of detecting their centuries-old origins. They are a living embodiment of the ancientness of Rome. The meaning of tradition is viewed in *Americans in Rome* as better preserved and more easily appreciable in the uses and mores of the people than in monuments and ruins. Antiquity loses then what Hildegard Eilert calls "its museum-like character" and becomes "sensually perceptible, recognizable in its original context and in its practical immediacy and dailiness" (1989, 83).

A painstaking portrayal of Rome's popular life is not merely instructive and useful but urgent as well. That life, Leland maintains, is destined to undergo a profound transformation. Many of its "noticeable traits" will inevitably vanish, and Rome, "no more the prolongation of the Middle Ages will be the capital of a nation earnestly striving with the present, and rapidly assuming its characteristics" (5). Though not overtly, the author of *Americans in Rome* claims for his work a relevance that has little to do with its literary value. The suggestion is that, by recording in writing something that will soon disappear, he has rendered a valuable service to posterity. Leland well exemplifies the kind of writing to which I referred in the Introduction, quoting Clifford's definition of "redemptive ethnography." "The other," Clifford maintains, "is lost, in disintegrating time and space, but saved in the text" (1986, 112), and it is as if the hidden message in Leland's preface had been decoded.

In *Americans in Rome,* the author's concern for the "vanishing other" also finds expression in his ambivalent attitude toward Italy's future. Often in the book does Leland envision an independent and unified Italy. With fervor, he foretells the end of the political power of the church and the transformation of the country into a modern lay state. Such a process is perceived by Leland as unfailingly accompanied by economic, social, and cultural progress, yet not devoid of sinister consequences. Thus it happens that while the most obsolete aspects of Italian life are negatively emphasized or exploited for their farcical potential, the prospect of change is at times anticipated with anxiety. In Leland's portrayal of the little mountain town of Segni, the arrival of modernity (symbolized, not surprisingly, by the railroad) wipes away not only ignorance, inefficiency, and superstition but cultural individuality as well. The town once conquered by Goths and Saracens faces new invasions which, though far less violent than those of old, are to Leland's eyes equally devastating.

On his way he passed a store having French calicoes in the window, and mourned in his heart to think how short a time it would be before these became popular, and the homemade picturesque dresses of the female Segnians would be discarded. The time, too, was fast coming — with the railroad from Rome to Naples — when travelers will overrun these mountain towns.... Then the peace of the Volscians will have departed, never, oh! never more to return. Then the women will wear — bonnets! and cheap French goods; will no longer ... bear aloft the graceful *conche* filled with sweet water from the fountain, for hydraulic rams will do their business. (241–42)[7]

# Afterword: Another Italy

American descriptions of modern, unified Italy are very different from those of the old, divided country we have encountered in the works discussed so far. In the concluding section of the present work, I shall refer briefly to a number of texts that I believe demonstrate this shift in the Americans' perception of Italian reality.

The prevailing impression given by the writings of American visitors to Italy after 1870, or in the period immediately preceding that date, is that some sort of major natural event had occurred — as if a natural barrier had collapsed and the peninsula had been inundated by modernity. It is as if the pulse of Italy, its rhythm of life, had unexpectedly started to accelerate at an alarming rate. The country that to many Americans had once seemed the perfect opposite of an increasingly industrialized and preeminently urban United States was now seen as being in danger of becoming too much like the land across the Atlantic.

One finds, as verification of this cultural shift, several expressions of bitterness, and even outrage, by those authors who witnessed the disfigurement of a part of Italy's architectural and natural patrimony, a phenomenon that accompanied the country's modernization. It is not surprising that many of them mourned the loss of ancient popular traditions, the abandonment of time-worn, idiosyncratic ways in favor of foreign or "international" fashions. One senses also, however, something that is not explicitly expressed: a feeling of resentment toward the young Italian nation for apparently divesting itself, quite thoughtlessly, of its role as *the* land of the picturesque.

The reaction to the changing scene of modern Italy suggests that of a spectator who has just learned that a long-awaited performance has been canceled. Not only does this attitude indicate that for the observer "what matters" about Italy is "its past, not present or future" (to use, once again,

James Clifford's phrase [1986, 113]), but also that any consequence of change is weighed more in terms of its impact on the country's foreign visitors, students, and admirers, than on its inhabitants. Exemplary, in this sense, is William Dean Howells's nostalgia (in *Italian Journeys*, published in 1867) for the time when "the happy wayfarer journeyed by vettura through the innumerable little states of the Peninsula" and had to show his or her passport "every other mile" (1988 [1867], 98–99). Through the warp of memory even the symbols of political division and repression (borders, customs offices, etc.) are transformed into pictorial or literary perceptions, factors important only in that they concur in the creation of a picturesque effect.

In *Italian Journeys*, as in most American books on Italy of the period, any modification of the Italian landscape is evaluated almost exclusively from an aesthetic point of view. Thus, for example, when the presence of railroads is referred to, what is emphasized is the clamor, or the smoke, of trains rather than their function as a means of transportation. A notable exception is, of course, Mark Twain's *The Innocents Abroad*. Indeed, Italy's brand new railways struck Twain as being among the very few subjects really worth admiring in the country. Yet even this apparently most unsentimental of travelers, having been startled by a "shrill whistle and the cry of 'All aboard — last train for Naples'" while immersed in the unearthly stillness of Pompeii, could not suppress his annoyance. The idea of "a railroad train actually running to old dead Pompeii ... was as strange a thing as one could imagine, and unpoetical and disagreeable as it was strange" (1910 [1869], 318).

Of all the accounts of the ways in which Italy changed as a nation, with Rome as its capital, none is more poignant and wistful than Henry James's *William Wetmore Story and His Friends* (1903). This book might easily be labeled a gallery of ghosts. In its pages, the reader encounters a series of figures who, together with the once famous sculptor and writer to whom the book is devoted, were part of the Anglo-American colony in nineteenth-century Italy. Yet, admirably evoked as many of them certainly are — consider only the magnificent section on Margaret Fuller — one feels that the most formidable ghost of all is not that of a human being but of a place: "old Italy" itself (and "old Rome," in particular). Reliving, as it were, the life of a long-time resident of Italy, James had a chance to experience, at least vicariously, the preunification scene that in real life he had only glimpsed (he made his first visit to Italy in 1869). The book is full of longing for the old times, when "Europe [and Italy in particular, I would add] was anything but easy" for Americans, because it was less known, less studied, less described, and far more different from America; far more "alien" than in James's age. William Wetmore Story and the other precursors of James's generation were then more explorers than simple travelers. A "chasm" (in James's words) divided them from their successors, especially considering that the years of change in Italy coincided with the post-Civil War period in the United States (1903, 1:4, 10). Neither country was ever to be the same again.

James was certainly not alone in his dissatisfaction with the present, in his effort to "cling to any touch — any echo of an echo ... that shows us, no matter for how few seconds, something of the old, the more human, way" (1903, 1:241–42). The regretful backward glance that characterizes his treatment of Story's Italian experience is also recognizable in the sculptor's own *Roba di Roma* (1862). In this work, Story pays homage to the old city he had known and loved before 1870, for in becoming the capital of the kingdom of Italy, Rome underwent nothing short of an urbanistic revolution. As is well known, broad thoroughfares were opened in the heart of the city, drastically changing a number of historical quarters and rows and rows of new buildings were built, more often than not at the expense of ancient landmarks, all of which aimed at making Rome fit the idea of a modern European capital. Readers browsing through one of the several reeditions of Story's popular book cannot fail to be struck by the many added footnotes which, in painful succession, inform them of the disappearance of beautiful villas, gardens, and other once-cherished spots.

Another possible reaction to the transformation of Rome was that of ignoring, at least in writing, the most conspicuous signs of change. This was the strategy of another American resident of Rome, the Italian-born novelist F. M. Crawford. In his Roman novels published between the mid-1880s and the beginning of this century, Crawford chose to recreate the papal Rome of his youth rather than the new capital of Italy. As Alessandra Contenti (1990) has pointed out, even when the action of these novels is contemporary with the time of their composition, the effects of modernization on the city are, whenever possible, left out of the picture. One significant exception is Crawford's *Don Orsino* (1892), in which the new face of Rome is exposed, only to be branded as ugly and vulgar. Here Crawford unhesitatingly shows us a city that has fallen into the hands of rapacious speculators — a city that, to use the words of one of his characters, has fallen "a victim to modern facts — which are not beautiful" (1895, 117). Talking of those who, like himself, are playing an active part in the edification of the new Rome, the same character says that they are "half Vandals and half Americans, and ... in a terrible hurry" (116).

One can safely maintain that before 1870 the word "hurry" was almost never associated with the Italian scene. In the eyes of many American travelers it seemed to be foreign to the country's vocabulary. What Crawford suggested in *Don Orsino* was that the "tempo" of Italy had changed and that the consequence might well be a progressive loss of cultural identity. In equating the rush toward modernity with barbarism and the American model, he was voicing the fears of many of his coun-trymen (on both sides of the Atlantic). Rome, and Italy by extension, was seen as being increasingly contaminated by those "economic or actual values" which, according to Henry Adams's description (1973 [1918], 90), had been unknown in the city of the popes before 1870.

Observing Florence and the Tuscan countryside at the close of the year 1869, Charles Eliot Norton described with lucid apprehension a country under the ever-increasing threat of cultural homologation, of conformity to the "commercial and trading taste, — the taste of New York and Paris." The "delightful individuality and expression of personal character" which in Italy, in his view, even the poorest houses in the most insignificant village possessed, were in danger of being obliterated forever, of disappearing, like the façade of many a building at the time, under a coat of neutral whitewash (1913, 1:369). Norton's concerns were far from being of a merely aesthetic nature. His attitude may be likened to that of a scholar who fears that the rare manuscript he is studying may be irremediably damaged. Believing it possible to study "national traits in doors and windows and balconies," he saw as a calamity the introduction in Italy of signs and values that were not the direct expression of the local culture. "I hate Americanism out of America" (1:372), Norton cried out in an 1869 letter written in Florence, words that were echoed in Henry B. Fuller's novel of 1886, *The Chevalier of Pensieri-Vani*. The example of America to older countries, a character in that book observed, served "less as a pattern than as a warning" (1890, 160).

Still, in Norton the alarm that the most arid features of contemporary American life might be reproduced in Italy coexisted somehow with the belief — or perhaps the hope — that the peninsula might still prove a formidable "'island' of resistance" (Salomone 1968, 1390) against the pressures of modernity. Possibly because of its rich variety of local traditions, its mosaic of cultural individualities, Italy seemed better equipped than other European countries to resist the invasion of what Norton called "'American' barbarism and ... universal materialism" (1913, 1:584). Celebrating, in 1870, the still intact medievalism of a city like Siena ("free from the taint of the ten per cent stock-broking age" [1:395]), Norton gave expression to that search for "alternatives" to "industrial capitalist society" which, as Jackson Lears has argued, was to become a major cultural phenomenon in the America of the late nineteenth and early twentieth centuries (Lears 1981, xi).

In Fuller's *The Chevalier of Pensieri-Vani,* the Abruzzi region is indicated as still primitive and unadulterated (1890, 94), further evidence of the tendency to characterize the central and southern areas of Italy as somewhat "immune" to the germ of modernity. To the movement back in time, toward medieval and premedieval days, there corresponded a geographical trajectory that progressively lowered the line separating old, supposedly "authentic" and "unspoiled" Italy from the new, industrial, "technological" and "Americanized" nation. It is significant that as early as 1864 the English poet Robert Browning, in a letter to William Wetmore Story, considered the possibility of a retreat toward the south to flee from the seemingly irresistible advance of the machine: "I am not sure ... that I might not incline to try the south, Naples or Sicily, when the railways overhaul Rome, as they seem likely to do" (James 1903, 2:152).

Examples of American writers commenting favorably on certain aspects of modern Italy are certainly not lacking. Yet one often notices, in such cases, that praise is given without great enthusiasm. Material improvements introduced in many cities by the government of unified Italy are duly referred to, but with a sort of cold benevolence, as if to imply that anything "material" or "actual" disagreed with the ideal image of the country. Even the conquest of liberty and independence could be viewed critically as an event bringing in its wake the unpleasantness of reality where before there lingered the enchantment of dream. Noticing that in postunification Rome the number of street singers and musicians, once so conspicuous, was dwindling day after day, William Wetmore Story concluded that "since Italy became a nation and Liberty has come in, Song has gone out" (1887, 39). As seen by Story, the achievement of nationhood in Italy appeared to have taken the form of a rite of passage, a sort of "coming of age" accompanied by a loss of innocence and spontaneity. It was a sadder and wiser country that had emerged from the long battle of the Risorgimento.

If in *William Wetmore Story and His Friends,* James lovingly resuscitated, albeit for a brief span of time, figures and scenes from a friend's, and a country's, past, in *Italian Hours* (1909) he attempted to give modern Italy its due. Though the pages of this book often brim with indignation at what the author calls the "villainous improvements" (1987, 28) of modern Italy, one also recognizes, on the part of the observer, a valiant effort to temper aesthetic and sentimental considerations and to suspend judgment on the results of change.

Confronted with the (to his eyes) disheartening effects of the restoration of St. Mark's in Venice, James seemed to appeal to his fellow travelers and devotees of Italy in rèmarking that "one must endeavor to believe that it is through innumerable lapses of taste that this deeply interesting country is groping her way to her place among the nations" (1987 [1909], 9). While decrying the "look of monstrous ... newness which distinguishes all the creations of the young Italian State," James acknowledges, on more than one occasion, the need to abandon the lofty stance of the spectator in order to grasp the full significance of what was happening around him. What is more, he is even capable, at a certain point, of looking at the Italian scene from a different perspective — of going, as it were, to the other end of the traveler's gaze: "Young Italy, preoccupied with its economical and political future, must be heartily tired of being admired for its eyelashes and its pose" (111). The author of *Italian Hours* even came to predict a thriving future for the young nation, but one in which, unlike in the past, there would no longer be room for the pursuit of both beauty and material success. Modern Italy would "equal, if not surpass, the most enterprising sections" of America, it would be a country "united and prosperous, but altogether scientific and commercial" (112).

The impression is that in James's vision the "Americanization" of Italy was to find expression in an abrupt breach with the past, in the development of a "museum mentality" towards the country's artistic tradition. In young Italy, the artistic achievements of the past would perhaps be efficiently restored and rejuvenated, but not matched. Modern Italians would demonstrate their proficiency not by creating new art but by guarding, preserving, and, like Hawthorne's Hilda, copying the works of the masters.

Though considerably less sorrowful in tone than *Italian Hours*, Edith Wharton's 1905 *Italian Backgrounds* also suggests that the time when Italian art "interpenetrated Italian life" was past (1989, 178). What char-acterizes Wharton's point of view is that while voicing her unhappiness at the differences between yesterday and today, she constantly empha-sizes the sheer abundance of what has been left intact of Italy's artistic riches. She tells of a country in which, undoubtedly, "the knife of modern improvement" (54) has cut deeply and left many scars, but where much remains that is worth the visitor's study and devotion. This also applies to nature, which, for the most part, is viewed as still unspoiled by the manifestations of "progress." It is characteristic of Wharton's pragmatic attitude towards the signs of modernity in Italy that in recalling a railway trip through the Tuscan countryside, she does not pause to comment on the irruption of the "machine" into such a landscape. The fact that she traveled by train is simply mentioned in passing; it is an unimportant detail, one that has no weight on the nature of the experience she is recreating on the page. What we find in *Italian Backgrounds* is certainly not the "deafening present" of James's story "The Madonna of the Future" (1908, 442), and even the most powerful embodiment of moder-nity, the train, cannot distract from the sensorial feast offered by the Italian scene.

Obviously, this brief afterword is not claiming to exhaust the analysis of the new American image of Italy as it emerged in the late 1860s. This, I believe, is a rich topic worthy of further research, particularly for its implications for the history of America's cultural response to modernity. As we have seen in the last chapter, Henry P. Leland believed that the very "difference" of Italy, the great distance that separated (not only in geographical terms) and distinguished it from the United States, made it function as the perfect "measure" of his native country's progress and achievements. Yet he also foresaw the time when that distance would be drastically reduced, when modernity (under the guise of French fashion, a sort of European anticipation of the coming American cultural invasion) would, so to speak, take over the Italian scene. For many of the

Americans who succeeded Leland in the "exploration" of Italy, the country's conquest of political independence and nationhood sadly coincided with the fulfillment of his prophecy.

# Notes

Unless otherwise indicated, the English translation of all foreign-language sources in this book is mine.

## Introduction

1. The expression "geographical denomination" was used by the Austrian Chancellor Prince von Metternich (1773–1859).

2. Viktor Hehn (1813–90) was a German scholar and the author of "Über die Physiognomie der italienischen Landschaft" [On the physiognomy of the Italian landscape], originally published in 1844, which he based on his travel impressions of 1839–40.

## Chapter 1

1. That Fuller's fears were grounded is demonstrated, for example, by a famous passage in Hawthorne's Italian journal. Relying only on second-hand sources, Hawthorne referred to Ossoli as "entirely ignorant even of his own language ... half an idiot ... [a] boor," and observed that the only possible explanation for Fuller's feelings toward him was that probably they had been "purely sensual" (1980, 155).

2. The moderate party advocated a federation of the Italian states under the presidency of the pope.

3. Dr. Samuel Gridley Howe (1801–76) was a philanthropist, a social reformer, and an antislavery activist.

4. In this chapter, all quotations from Howe's *Passion Flowers* are from the 1854 Ticknor, Reed, and Fields edition.

5. For an illuminating analysis of *Summer on the Lakes* and other significant examples of women's writing about the frontier, see Annette Kolodny's *The Land Before Her* (1984, 112–30).

6. Fuller's dispatches for *The New York Tribune* are included in *At Home and Abroad, or Things and Thoughts in America and Europe*. In this chapter, all quotations from this work are from the 1971 Kennikat Press edition.

7. In his letter, Mazzini exhorted Pius IX to become the spiritual leader of the movement for a unified Italy.

8. The excommunication was intended for all those individuals who had contributed to the overthrow of the pope's temporal authority.

9. During her stay in Rome, Howe took Hebrew lessons from a learned rabbi of the ghetto.

10. On 30 April 1849 (the day in which the siege of Rome began), Fuller was named superintendent of the Hospital of the Fate Bene Fratelli.

11. At the outbreak of the 1848 insurrection of Milan, Princess Belgioioso was in Naples, where she hired a steamship to carry a battalion of volunteers to the capital of Lombardy.

## Chapter 2

1. In this chapter, all quotations from *The Marble Faun* are from the 1986 Ohio State University Press edition.

2. Also absent between these two characters is that nonverbal communication — a pattern of gazes, movements and gestures — which, as John L. Idol (1991) has indicated, is a prominent feature of *The Marble Faun*.

3. Writing on the "uses of primitivism" in *The Marble Faun*, Nancy Bentley has argued that "the Roman Catholic clergyman served as America's Old World savage, an animal-like character whose features displayed his depravity" (1990, 916).

## Chapter 3

1. The Bautta is a usually black or white mouthless mask that is still used in Venice during the Carnival.

2. Cooper's main sources for plot and characters were William Dunlap's translation of J. H. D. Zschokke's play *Abaellino the Great Bandit* (1801) and M. G. Lewis's translation of Zschokke's novel *Abaellino the Bravo of Venice* (1804).

3. Another example of Cooper's imagination at work in the recreation of an Italian landscape is *The Wing-and-Wing* (1842). The first part of this novel is set on the island of Elba, where Cooper spent less than a day.

4. Rosella Mamoli Zorzi has pointed out that "the painterly method of chiaroscuro dominates the method of description" (1990, 294) in *The Bravo*.

5. In this chapter, all quotations from *The Bravo* are from the 1963 College & University edition.

6. Andrew M. Canepa has noted how, in eighteenth-century British travel accounts, the political and economic decline of Venice was seen as coinciding with the emergence of "a certain proficiency in staging spectacles" (1972, 122). Significantly enough, Canepa quotes from a letter in which the actor David Garrick comments that the Venetians "were as little formidable in war & Politicks, as they were superior to all ye World as Managers of a Puppet-Shew" ( 122).

7.  Interestingly enough, "Monaldi" is also the title (from the name of the protagonist) of Washington Allston's Italian novel. Written in 1822, it was published in 1841.

8.  In 1871, in a letter to John Ruskin, Charles Eliot Norton singled out Venice as the Italian city in which most impressive and painful was the difference between the days of greatness and those of decadence: "In other cities even where there is more ruin, as in Rome, or where the political change has been as great, as in Florence, there is no such complete moral and social gulf between present and past" (1913, 1:406).

9.  Venice is also the setting of Howells's novels *A Foregone Conclusion* (1875), *The Lady of the Aroostook* (1879), and *A Fearful Responsibility* (1881).

10.  In this chapter, all quotations from *Venetian Life* are from the 1867 Hard and Houghton reprint.

11.  Like Cooper and, later, Twain, Howells follows Goethe's example in identifying the gondola with the hearse. This parallel, according to Giorgio Cusatelli, expresses the "anthropological-cultural relation between travel and death" (1987, 92).

# Chapter 4

1.  In this chapter, all quotations from Henry Tuckerman's *The Italian Sketch Book* are from the 1837 reprint.

2.  In this chapter, all quotations from *Americans in Rome* are from the 1863 Charles T. Evans edition.

3.  In 1863, four years after his return from Europe, Leland was seriously injured in the Civil War.

4.  On the reaction of English and American travelers to the novitiate ceremony, see Michèle Rivas's 1979 *Les écrivains anglais et americains à Rome et l'image litteraire de la société romaine contemporaine de 1800 à 1870*, pp. 337–38.

5.  Of particular interest with regard to Italian culture is Tuckerman's detailed description (complete with plot summary and citations in Italian) of Vincenzo Bellini's *Norma* (first performed on 12 December 1831 in Milan) (1837, 71–75).

6.  For an analysis of Greenough's theories, see Matthiessen 1968, 140–52.

7.  As Ruggiero Romano has noted in *Paese Italia* (1994), the first signs of the diffusion of French taste in clothing appeared in Venice toward the end of the eighteenth century (6).

# Bibliography

Adams, Henry. 1973. *The Education of Henry Adams*. Edited by Ernest Samuels. 1918. Reprint, Boston: Houghton Mifflin Company.

Adams, Percy. 1983. *Travel Literature and the Evolution of the Novel*. Lexington: The University Press of Kentucky.

Alfani, Augusto. 1878. *Il carattere degli italiani*. Florence: G. Barberà.

Allston, Washington. 1841. *Monaldi: A Tale*. Boston: Charles C. Little and James Brown.

Ambrosini, Federica. 1975. "Un incontro mancato: Venezia e Stati Uniti d'America (1776–1797)." *Archivio Veneto* 140: 123–71.

Andersen, Hans Christian. 1890. *The Improvisatore*. Translated by Mary Howitt. Boston: Houghton Mifflin Company.

Anderson, Benedict. 1983. *Imagined Communities*. London: Verso.

Angelini, Giulia. 1990. "The Significance of Italian History in Howells's Work." *Annali di Ca' Foscari* 28.1–2: 5–17.

Anicetti, Luigi. 1957. "William D. Howells, Console a Venezia." *Nuova Rivista Storica* 41: 87–106.

———. 1968. *Scrittori inglesi e americani a Venezia (1816–1960)*. Treviso, Italy: Canova.

Arvin, Newton. 1942. "Toward the Whole Evidence on Melville as a Lecturer." *American Notes and Queries* 2: 21–22.

Asad, Talal. 1986. "The Concept of Cultural Translation in British Social Anthropology." In *Writing Culture: The Poetics and Politics of Ethnography*, edited by James Clifford and George E. Marcus. Berkeley: University of California Press.

Baker, Paul R. 1964. *The Fortunate Pilgrims: Americans in Italy 1800–1860*. Cambridge, Mass.: Harvard University Press.

Balandier, Georges. 1973. *Le società comunicanti*. Translated by S. Brilli Cattarini and R. Scacchi. Bari, Italy: Laterza.

Barbieri, Gaetano. 1835. Review of *The Bravo*, by James Fenimore Cooper. *Raccoglitore Italiano e Straniero*. Quoted in Emilio Goggio, "Cooper's *Bravo* in Italy," *The Romanic Review* 20 (1929): 222–30.

Battafarano, Italo Michele. 1989. "La *Fisionomia del paesaggio italiano* secondo Viktor Hehn (1844)." In *Viaggi in Utopia e altri luoghi,* edited by M. Enrica D'Agostini. Milan: Guerini e Associati.

Battilana, Marilla. 1989. "I viaggiatori del mondo anglosassone: inglesi e americani." In *Venezia dei grandi viaggiatori*, by Alvise Zorzi, Emanuele Kanceff, Marilla Battilana, Francis Claudon, Piero Cazzola, and Gianni Carlo Sciolla. Casale Monferrato, Italy: Edizioni Abete.

Baym, Nina. 1976. *The Shape of Hawthorne's Career*. Ithaca, N.Y.: Cornell University Press.

Beales, Derek. 1971. *The Risorgimento and the Unification of Italy*. London: George Allen & Unwin Ltd.

Bensick, Carol Marie. 1985. *La Nouvelle Beatrice*. New Brunswick, N.J.: Rutgers University Press.

Bentley, Nancy. 1990. "Slaves and Fauns: Hawthorne and the Uses of Primitivism." *ELH* 4: 901–37.

Bercovitch, Sacvan. 1968. "Of Wise and Foolish Virgins: Hilda Versus Miriam in Hawthorne's *The Marble Faun*." *New England Quarterly* 41: 281–86.

Berger, John. 1977. *Ways of Seeing*. Harmondsworth, England: Penguin.

Bewley, Marius. 1959. *The Eccentric Design; Form in the Classic American Novel*. New York: Columbia University Press.

Bisutti, Francesca. 1984–85. "The Sad Nymph of Margaret Fuller: A Description for a Besieged City." *Rivista di studi anglo-americani* 3: 557–64.

Bocca, Giorgio. 1990. *La Dis-unità d'Italia*. Milan: Garzanti.

Bollati, Giulio. 1989. "L'italiano." In *Storia d'italia Einaudi: I caratteri originali*, edited by Ruggiero Romano and Corrado Vivanti, vol. 2. Turin, Italy: Einaudi.

Borges, Jorge Luis. 1960. *Otras Inquisiciones*. Buenos Aires: Emecé.

Borgese, Elisabeth Mann, ed. 1961. *Testimonianze americane sull'Italia del Risorgimento*. Milan: Edizioni di Comunità.

Borghese, Lucia. 1987. "Il viaggio in Italia di Karl Hillebrand." In *La letteratura di viaggio*, edited by M. Enrica D'Agostini. Milan: Guerini e Associati.

Brandi, Cesare. 1986. *Segno e immagine*. Palermo, Italy: Aesthetica.

Brooks, Van Wick. 1958. *The Dream of Arcadia: American Writers and Artists in Italy 1760–1915*. New York: E. P. Dutton & Co.

_____. 1959. *Howells: His Life and World*. New York: E. P. Dutton & Co.

Brown, Arthur W. 1964. *Margaret Fuller*. New York: Twayne Pubs.

Bryant, William Cullen. 1850. *Letters of a Traveller: Or, Notes of Things Seen in Europe and America*. New York: G. P. Putnam.

Burke, Edmund. 1986. *A Philosophical Enquiry into the Origin of Our Ideas of the Sublime and Beautiful*. 1757. Reprint. Notre Dame, Ind.: University of Notre Dame Press.

Cady, Edwin H. 1953. "William Dean Howells in Italy: Some Bibliographical Notes." *Symposium* 7: 147–53.

Cady, Edwin H., and Norma W. Cady, eds. 1983. *Critical Essays on W. D. Howells, 1866–1920*. Boston, Mass.: G. K. Hall & Co.

Canepa, Andrew M. 1972. "From Degenerate Scoundrel to Noble Savage: The Italian Stereotype in 18th-century British Travel Literature." *English Miscellany* 22: 107–46.

Cecioni, Cesare G. 1965. "La prima esperienza italiana di William Dean Howells." *Siculorum Gymnasium* 18: 93–119.

Chaney, Edward. 1984. "The Grand Tour and Beyond: British and American Travellers in Southern Italy 1545–1960." In *Oxford, China, and Italy*, edited by Edawrd Chaney and Neil Ritchie. London: Thames and Hudson.

Chevigny, Bell Gale. 1976. *The Woman and the Myth, Margaret Fuller's Life and Writings*. Old Westbury, N.Y.: The Feminist Press.

Clifford, Deborah P. 1979. *Mine Eyes Have Seen the Glory, A Biography of Julia Ward Howe*. Boston: Little, Brown and Co., The Atlantic Monthly Press.

Clifford, James. 1986. "On Ethnographic Allegory." In *Writing Culture: The Poetics and Politics of Ethnography*, edited by James Clifford and George E. Marcus. Berkeley:

University of California Press.

Conrad, Susan Phinney. 1979. *Perish the Thought: Intellectual Women in Romantic America, 1830–1860*. New York: Oxford University Press.

Contenti, Alessandra. 1990. "La topografia del rimpianto: Roma al tempo di Pio IX nei romanzi di F. Marion Crawford." *Rivista di studi anglo-americani* 8: 315–26.

Cooper, James Fenimore. 1896. *The Wing-and-Wing*. 1842. Reprint, New York: G. B. Putnam's Sons.

_____. 1963. *The Bravo*. Edited by Donald A. Ringe. 1831. Reprint, New Haven, Conn.: College & University Press.

_____. 1981. *Gleanings in Europe: Italy*. Edited by John Conron and Constance Ayers Denne. 1837. Reprint, Albany: State University of New York Press.

Crapanzano, Vincent. 1986. "Hermes' Dilemma: The Masking of Subversion in Ethnographic Description." In *Writing Culture: The Poetics and Politics of Ethnography*, edited by James Clifford and George E. Marcus. Berkeley: University of California Press.

Crawford, Francis Marion. 1884. *A Roman Singer*. New York: Macmillan.

_____. 1887. *Marzio's Crucifix*. New York: Macmillan.

_____. 1887. *Saracinesca*. New York: Macmillan.

_____. 1889. *Sant'Ilario*. New York: Macmillan.

_____. 1893. *Pietro Ghisleri*. New York: Macmillan.

_____. 1895. *Casa Braccio*. 2 vols. New York: Macmillan.

_____. 1895. *Don Orsino*. 1892. Reprint, New York: Macmillan.

_____. 1902. *Cecilia: A Story of Modern Rome*. New York: Macmillan.

_____. 1903. *The Heart of Rome: A Tale of the "Lost Water."* London: Macmillan.

_____. 1904. *Whosoever Shall Offend*. New York: Macmillan.

_____. 1906. *A Lady of Rome*. New York: Macmillan.

Croce, Benedetto. 1949. *Filosofia e storiografia*. Bari, Italy: Laterza.

Cusatelli, Giorgio. 1987. "I viaggi italiani dei tedeschi nel XVIII secolo." In *La letteratura di viaggio*, edited by Maria Enrica d'Agostini. Milan: Guerini e associati.

Da Ponte, Lorenzo. 1918. *Memorie*. 2 vols. Bari, Italy: Laterza.

Daru, Pierre Antoine Noël Bruno. 1853. *Histoire de la République de Venise*. 7 vols. 1829. Reprint, Paris: Firmin Didot frères.

De Mauro, Tullio. 1963. *Storia linguistica dell'Italia unita*. Bari, Italy: Laterza.

De Puy, Harry. 1984. "*The Marble Faun*: Another Portrait of Margaret Fuller?" *Arizona Quarterly* 40.2: 163–78.

De Staël, Madame. 1894. *Corinne; or Italy*. 2 vols. London: Dent & Co.

Dean, James L. 1970. *Howells's Travels toward Art*. Albuquerque: University of New Mexico Press.

Deiss, Joseph Jay. 1969. *The Roman Years of Margaret Fuller*. New York: Crowell.

Dekker, George, and John P. McWilliams, eds. 1985. *Fenimore Cooper: The Critical Heritage*. London: Routledge & Kegan Paul.

Del Negro, Piero, and Federica Ambrosini. 1989. *L'aquila e il leone: I contatti diplomatici per un accordo commerciale fra gli Stati Uniti d'America e la Repubblica Veneta, 1783–1797*. Padua, Italy: Programma e 1+1 Editori.

Del Negro, Piero. 1986. *Il mito americano nella Venezia del'700*. Padua, Italy: Liviana Editrice.

Detti, Emma. 1942. *Margaret Fuller Ossoli e i suoi corrispondenti*. Florence: Le Monnier.

Earnest, Ernest. 1968. *Expatriates and Patriots: American Artists, Scholars, and Writers in Europe*. Durham, N.C.: Duke University Press.

Eilert, Hildegard. 1989. "Wilhelm Müller, 'Professore di Scienza plebea' in Italia." In *Viaggi in Utopia e altri luoghi*, edited by Maria Enrica D'Agostini. Milan: Guerini e Associati.

Fink, Guido. 1990. "Eppur si muove! The American Rome as Text." *Rivista di studi anglo-americani* 8: 301–14.

Fuller, Henry B. 1890. *The Chevalier of Pensieri-Vani*. 1886. Reprint, Boston: J. G. Cupples.

Fuller, Margaret. 1852. *Memoirs of Margaret Fuller Ossoli*. Edited by J. F. Clarke, R. W. Emerson, and W. H. Channing. 2 vols. Boston: Phillips, Sampson.

———. 1971. *At Home and Abroad, or Things and Thoughts in America and Europe*. 1856. Reprint, Port Washington, N.Y.: Kennikat Press.

———. 1903. *Love Letters of Margaret Fuller*. Edited by Julia Ward Howe. New York: Appleton.

———. 1988. *The Letters of Margaret Fuller*. Edited by Robert N. Hudspeth. Vols. 4–5. Ithaca, N.Y.: Cornell University Press.

———. 1991. *Summer on the Lakes, in 1843*. 1844. Reprint, Urbana and Chicago: University of Illinois Press.

Gadda Conti, Giuseppe. 1971. *William Dean Howells*. Rome: Edizioni di storia e letteratura.

Geertz, Clifford. 1973. *The Interpretation of Cultures*. New York: Basic Books.

Gioberti, Vincenzo. 1846. *Del Primato morale e civile degli italiani*. 2 vols. 1843. Reprint, Capolago, Italy.

Goethe, Johann Wolfgang. 1921. *Le elegie, le epistole e gli epigrammi veneziani*. Translated by Guido Manacorda. 1790. Reprint. Florence: Sansoni.

———. 1987. *Italian Journey*. Translated by W. H. Auden and Elizabeth Mayer. 1789. Reprint, Harmondsworth, England: Penguin Books.

Goggio, Emilio. 1929. "Cooper's *Bravo* in Italy." *The Romanic Review* 20: 222–30.

Goldman, Arnold. 1984. "The Plot of Hawthorne's *The Marble Faun*." *Journal of American Studies* 18: 383–404.

Grant, Mary H. 1982. *Private Woman, Public Person: An Account of the Life of Julia Ward Howe from 1819 to 1888*. Ann Arbor, Mich.: University Microfilms International.

Greeley, Horace. 1869. *Recollections of a Busy Life*. New York: J. B. Ford & Co.

Grube, Alberta Fabris. 1969. "La trilogia europea di J. F. Cooper." *Studi americani* 15: 33–60.

Hawthorne, Nathaniel. 1962. *The Scarlet Letter*. Edited by William Charvat, Roy Harvey Pearce, Claude M. Simpson, Fredson Bowers, and Matthew J. Bruccoli. 1850. Reprint, Columbus: Ohio State University Press.

———. 1974. "Rappaccini's Daughter." In *Mosses from an Old Manse*, edited by William Charvat, Roy Harvey Pearce, Claude M. Simpson, Fredson Bowers, L. Neal Smith, John Manning, and J. Donald Crowley. 1846. Reprint, Columbus: Ohio State University Press.

———. 1986. *The Marble Faun*. Edited by William Charvat, Roy Harvey Pearce, Claude M. Simpson, Matthew J. Bruccoli, Fredson Bowers, and L. Neal Smith. 1860. Reprint, Columbus: Ohio State University Press.

———. 1980. *The French and Italian Notebooks*. Edited by Thomas Woodson. 1871. Reprint, Columbus: Ohio State University Press.

———. 1987. *The Letters*. Vols. 17–18. Edited by Thomas Woodson, James A. Rabino,

L. Neal Smith, and Norman Holmes Pearson. Columbus: Ohio State University Press.

Hehn, Viktor. 1908. "Über die Physiognomie der italianischen Landschaft (1844)." In *Aus baltischer Geistesarbeit. Reden und Aufsätze*. Riga: Deutschen Verein in Livland.

Hobsbawm, E. J. 1990. *Nations and Nationalism since 1780: Programme, Myth, Reality*. Cambridge: Cambridge University Press.

Howe, Julia Ward. 1854. *Passion Flowers*. Boston: Ticknor, Reed and Fields.

_____. 1883. *Margaret Fuller*. Boston: Roberts Brothers.

_____. 1899. *Reminiscences*. Boston: Houghton, Mifflin and Co.

Howells, William Dean. 1864. "Recent Italian Comedy." *North American Review* 99: 364–401.

_____. 1988. *Italian Journeys*. 1867. Reprint, Marlboro, Vt.: The Marlboro Press.

_____. 1867. *Venetian Life*. New York: Hard and Houghton.

_____. 1875. *A Foregone Conclusion*. Boston: J. R. Osgood.

_____. 1879. *The Lady of the Aroostook*. Boston: Houghton, Mifflin.

_____. 1881. *A Fearful Responsibility*. Boston: J. R. Osgood.

_____. 1887. *Modern Italian Poets*. New York: Harper & Brothers.

Hughes, H. Stuart. 1965. *The United States and Italy*. Cambridge, Mass.: Harvard University Press.

Idol, John L. 1991. "'A Linked Circle of Three' Plus One: Nonverbal Communication in *The Marble Faun*." *Studies in the Novel* 1: 139–51.

Irving, Washington. 1978. *The Sketch Book*. Edited by Haskell Springer. 1820. Reprint, Boston: Twayne Publishers.

_____. 1987. *Tales of a Traveller*. Edited by Judith Gibling Haig. Boston: Twayne Publishers.

Jackson, J. B. 1980. *The Necessity for Ruins*. Amherst, Mass.: University of Massachusetts Press.

James, Henry. 1880. *Hawthorne*. New York: Harper & Brothers.

_____. 1903. *William Wetmore Story and His Friends*. 2 vols. New York: Grove Press.

_____. 1987. *Italian Hours*. 1909. Reprint, New York: The Ecco Press.

_____. 1908. "The Madonna of the Future." In *The Novels and Tales of Henry James*, vol. 13. New York: Charles Scribner's Sons.

_____. 1946. *The American Scene*. Edited by W. H. Auden. New York: Charles Scribner's Sons.

_____. 1971. "The Aspern Papers." In *The Spoils of Poynton and Other Stories*. New York: Doubleday & Co.

_____. 1971. "Daisy Miller." In *The Spoils of Poynton and Other Stories*. New York: Doubleday & Co.

_____. 1978. *The Wings of the Dove*. New York: W. W. Norton & Co.

_____. 1980. *Roderick Hudson*. Oxford: Oxford University Press.

Jarves, James Jackson. 1856. *Italian Sights and Papal Principles, Seen Through American Spectacles*. New York: Harper & Brothers.

Johnston, William M. 1987. *In Search of Italy; Foreign Writers in Northern Italy Since 1800*. University Park and London: Pennsylvania State University Press.

Kasson, Joy S. 1982. *Artistic Voyagers: Europe and the American Imagination in the Works of Irving, Allston, Cole, Cooper, and Hawthorne*. Westport, Conn.: Greenwood Press.

Kirkland, Caroline M. 1849. *Holidays Abroad; or Europe From the West*. 2 vols. New York: Baker and Scribner.

Kolodny, Annette. 1984. *The Land Before Her; Fantasy and Experience of the American*

*Frontiers, 1630–1860*. Chapel Hill and London: University of North Carolina Press.

Kuon, Peter. 1987. "A che ti serve, allora, tanto viaggiare? Il viaggio come metafora semiologica in *Le città invisibili* di Italo Calvino." In *La letteratura di viaggio*, edited by M. Enrica D'Agostini. Milan: Guerini e Associati.

La Piana, Angelina. 1938. *La cultura americana e l'Italia*. Turin, Italy: Einaudi.

Lears, Jackson. 1981. *No Place of Grace: Antimodernism and the Transformation of American Culture 1880–1920*. New York: Pantheon Books.

Leland, Henry P. 1863. *Americans in Rome*. New York: Charles T. Evans.

Lévi-Strauss, Claude. 1964. *Tristes Tropiques*. Translated by John Russell. New York: Atheneum.

Levine, Harry. 1964. "Statues from Italy: *The Marble Faun*." In *Hawthorne Centenary Essays*, edited by Roy Harvey Pearce. Columbus: Ohio State University Press.

Levine, Robert S. 1990. "Antebellum Rome in *The Marble Faun*." *American Literary History* 2.1: 19–38.

Liebman, Sheldon W. 1967. "The Design of *The Marble Faun*." *New England Quarterly* 40: 61–78.

Mack Smith, Denis. 1968. *The Making of Italy, 1796–1870*. New York: Walker.

Manzoni, Alessandro. 1969. *I promessi sposi*. Edited by Luigi Russo. Florence: La nuova Italia.

Marcelli, Umberto. 1970. *Interpretazioni del risorgimento*. Bologna: Patron.

Marder, Daniel. 1984. *Exiles at Home: A Story of Literature in Nineteenth Century America*. New York: University Press of America.

Marraro, Howard R. 1932. *American Opinion on the Unification of Italy*. New York: Columbia University Press.

———. 1943. "Unpublished American Documents on the Roman Republic of 1849." *Catholic History Review* 28: 459–90.

———. 1944. "American Travelers in Rome, 1840–1850." *Catholic History Review* 29: 470–509.

Matthiessen, F. O. 1968. *American Renaissance: Art and Expression in the Age of Emerson and Whitman*. Oxford: Oxford University Press.

Mazzini, Giuseppe. 1950. *Dei doveri dell'uomo*. 1845. Reprint, Milan: Rizzoli.

McCarthy, Harold T. 1968. "Hawthorne's Dialogue with Rome: *The Marble Faun*." *Studi Americani* 14: 97–112.

Melville, Herman. 1987. "Statues in Rome." In *The Piazza Tales and Other Prose Pieces 1839–1860*, edited by Harrison Hayford, Alma A. Mac Dougall, and Thomas Tanselle. 1857. Reprint, Chicago: Northwestern University Press.

———. 1955. *Journal of a Visit to Europe and the Levant: October 11, 1856–May 6, 1857*. Edited by Howard C. Horsford. Princeton, N.J.: Princeton University Press.

Mileur, Jean-Pierre. 1990. *The Critical Romance: The Critic as Reader, Writer, Hero*. Madison: University of Wisconsin Press.

Miller, Perry, ed. 1963. *Margaret Fuller, American Romantic*. New York: Anchor Books.

Myerson, Joel, ed. 1980. *Critical Essays on Margaret Fuller*. Boston: G. K. Hall.

Nevius, Blake. 1976. *Cooper's Landscapes, An Essay on the Picturesque Vision*. Berkeley: University of California Press.

Norton, Charles Eliot. 1859. *Notes of Travel and Study in Italy*. Boston: Ticknor and Fields.

———. 1913. *Letters of Charles Eliot Norton*. 2 vols. Edited by Sara Norton and M. A. DeWolfe Howe. Boston: Houghton Mifflin.

Paris, Bernard J. 1956. "Optimism and Pessimism in *The Marble Faun*" *Boston*

*University Studies in English* 2: 95–112.

Pattison, Joseph C. 1963. "The Guilt of the Innocent Donatello." *Emerson Society Quarterly* 31.2: 66–68.

Pearce, Roy Harvey. 1988. *Savagism and Civilization: A Study of the Indian and the American Mind.* Berkeley: University of California Press.

Perosa, Sergio. 1979. *L'Euro-America di Henry James.* Vicenza, Italy: Neri Pozza.

Peterson, Roy Merel. 1932. "Echoes of the Italian Risorgimento in Contemporary American Writers." *PMLA* 47: 220–40.

Pine-Coffin, R. S., ed. 1974. *Bibliography of British and American Travel in Italy to 1860.* Florence: Leo S. Olschki.

Pinto-Surdi, Alessandra. 1984. *Americans in Rome, 1764–1860: A Descriptive Catalogue of the Exhibition Held in the Palazzo Antici Mattei....* Rome: Centro Studi Americani.

Prezzolini, Giuseppe. 1971. *Come gli americani scoprirono l'Italia.* Bologna: Massimiliano Boni.

Ragionieri, Ernesto. 1969. *Italia giudicata, 1861–1945, ovvero la storia degli italiani scritta dagli altri.* Bari, Italy: Laterza.

Railton, Stephen. 1978. *Fenimore Cooper: A Study of His Life and Imagination.* Princeton, N.J.: Princeton University Press.

Remotti, Francesco. 1990. *Noi primitivi: lo specchio dell'antropologia.* Turin, Italy: Bollati Boringhieri.

Richards, Laura E., and Maude Howe Elliot. 1916. *Julia Ward Howe, 1819–1910.* 2 vols. Boston: Houghton Mifflin.

Richardson, Edgar P., and Otto Wittmann. 1951. *Travelers in Arcadia: American Artists in Italy, 1830–1875.* Detroit, Mich.: Detroit Institute of Art.

Ringe, Donald A. 1958. "James Fenimore Cooper and Thomas Cole: An Analogous Technique." *American Literature* 30: 26–36.

———. 1963. Introduction to *The Bravo,* by James Fenimore Cooper. New Haven, Conn.: College & University Press.

———. 1990 "Go East, Young Man, and Discover Your Country." *The Kentucky Review* 10.1: 3–20.

Rivas, Michèle. 1979. *Les écrivains anglais et americains à Rome et l'image litteraire de la société romaine contemporaine de 1800 à 1870.* Paris: Université de la Sorbonne, Atelier National de Reproduction des Théses.

Romano, Ruggiero. 1994. *Paese Italia: venti secoli d'identità.* Rome: Donzelli.

Rostemberg, Leona. 1940. "Margaret Fuller's Roman Diary." *Journal of Modern History* 12: 209–20.

Said, Edward. 1991. *Orientalism: Western Conceptions of the Orient.* Harmondsworth, England: Penguin Books.

Salomone, William A. 1968. "The 19th Century Discovery of Italy: An Essay in American Cultural History." *American Historical Review* 73: 1359–91.

Schumaker, Conrad. 1984. "'A Daughter of the Puritans': History in Hawthorne's *The Marble Faun.*" *New England Quarterly* 57: 65–83.

Scrimgeour, Gary J. 1964. "The Marble Faun: Hawthorne's Faery Land." *American Literature* 36: 271–87.

Sealts, Merton M. 1957. *Melville as Lecturer.* Cambridge, Mass.: Harvard University Press.

Soria, Regina. 1982. *Dictionary of Nineteenth-Century American Artists in Italy 1760–1914.* East Brunswick, N.J.: Associated University Presses and Fairleigh Dickinson University Press.

Spengemann, William. 1977. *The Adventurous Muse*. New Haven, Conn.: Yale University Press.

Spini, G., A. M. Mastellone, R. Luraghi, T. Bonazzi, and R. Ruffilli. 1976. *Italia e America dal Settecento all'eta' dell'imperialismo*. Venice: Marsilio.

Story, William Wetmore. 1885. *Fiammetta*. Boston: Houghton Mifflin.

_____. 1887. *Roba di Roma*. 2 vols. 1862. Reprint, Boston and New York: Houghton Mifflin.

Stowe, Harriet Beecher. 1863. *Agnes of Sorrento*. Boston: Houghton Mifflin.

Strout, Cushing. 1963. *The American Image of the Old World*. New York: Harper & Row.

Tabucchi, Antonio. 1990. "Una, dieci, cento Toscane." *Meridiani* May: 8–13.

Tharp, Louise Hall. 1956. *Three Saints and a Sinner: Julia Ward Howe, Louisa, Annie and Sam Ward*. Boston: Little, Brown.

Todorov, Tzvetan. 1989. *Poetica della prosa*. Translated by Elisabetta Ceciarelli. Rome: Theoria.

Tuckerman, Henry T. 1837. *The Italian Sketch Book*. 1835. Reprint, Boston: Light & Stearns. A third edition, conspicuously augmented and revised, came out in 1848.

_____. 1839. *Isabel, or Sicily*. Philadelphia: Lea and Blanchard.

_____. 1841. *Rambles and Reveries*. New York: James P. Giffing.

Turri, Eugenio. 1979. *Semiologia del paesaggio italiano*. Milan: Longanesi & Co.

_____. 1983. *Antropologia del paesaggio*. Milan: Edizioni di Comunità.

Twain, Mark. 1910. *The Innocents Abroad*. 1869. Reprint, London, Melbourne, and Toronto: Ward Lock & Co.

Vance, William L. 1990. *America's Rome*. 2 vols. New Haven, Conn.: Yale University Press.

Venturi, Franco. 1973. "L'Italia fuori d'Italia." In *Storia d'Italia Einaudi*, vol. 3. Turin, Italy: Einaudi.

Wegelin, Cristof. 1947. "Europe in Hawthorne's Fiction" *ELH* 14: 219–45.

Wharton, Edith. 1989. *Italian Backgrounds*. 1905. Reprint, New York: The Ecco Press.

Wittman, Otto, Jr. 1952. "The Italian Experience (American Artists in Italy 1830–1875)." *American Quarterly* 4: 3–15.

Woodress, James L. 1952. *Howells & Italy*. Durham, N.C.: Duke University Press.

Woolson, Constance Fenimore. 1895. *The Front Yard and Other Italian Stories*. New York: Harper & Brothers.

Wright, Nathalia. 1965. *American Novelists in Italy: The Discoverers: Allston to James*. Philadelphia: University of Pennsylvania Press.

Wynne, George. 1966. *Early Americans in Rome*. Rome: Daily American Printing Co.

Zorzi, Pietro. 1835. "Osservazioni sul *Bravo*, romanzo storico del Sign. James Fenimore Cooper." *L'indicatore Lombardo* January: 1–8. Venice: Stamperia Pirrotta.

Zorzi, Rosella Mamoli. 1986. Introduction to *Un'americana a Roma, 1847–49,* by Margaret Fuller, and translated by Rosella Mamoli Zorzi and Cristina Malagutti. Pordenone, Italy: Edizioni Studio Tesi.

_____. 1990. "The Text is the City: The Representation of Venice in Two Tales by Irving and Poe and a Novel by Cooper." *Rivista di studi anglo-americani* 8: 285–300.

Zschokke, J. H. D. 1972. *The Bravo of Venice*. Translated by M. G. Lewis. 1804. Reprint, New York: Arno Press.

_____. 1820. *Abaellino the Great Bandit*. Translated by William Dunlap. New York: T. Longworth.

# Index

113

# DATE DUE

| OCT 01 1996 | | | |
|---|---|---|---|
| ~~JAN 0 2 2003~~ | | | |
| | | | |
| | | | |
| | | | |
| | | | |
| | | | |
| | | | |
| | | | |
| | | | |
| | | | |
| | | | |
| | | | |
| | | | |
| | | | |
| | | | |
| | | | |